# CRITICAL ACCLAIM FOR *TRAVELERS' TALES*

"The *Travelers' Tales* series is quite remarkable."
—Jan Morris, author of *Journeys*, *Locations*, and *Hong Kong*

"For the thoughtful traveler, these books are an invaluable resource. There's nothing like them on the market."
—Pico Iyer, author of *Video Night in Kathmandu*

"The *Travelers' Tales* series should become required reading for anyone visiting a foreign country who wants to truly step off the tourist track and experience another culture, another place, first hand."
—Nancy Paradis, *St. Petersburg Times*

"...*Travelers' Tales* is a valuable addition to any pre-departure reading list."
—Tony Wheeler, publisher, Lonely Planet Publications

"I can't think of a better way to get comfortable with a destination than by delving into *Travelers' Tales*...before reading a guidebook, before seeing a travel agent. The series helps visitors refine their interests and readies them to communicate with the peoples they come in contact with...."
—Paul Glassman, Society of American Travel Writers

"This is the stuff memories can be duplicated from."
—Karen Krebsbach, *Foreign Service Journal*

"Like having been there, done it, seen it. If there's one thing traditional guidebooks lack, it's the really juicy travel information, the personal stories about back alleys and brief encounters. The *Travelers' Tales* series fills this gap with an approach that's all anecdotes, no directions."
—Jim Gullo, *Diversion*

TRAVELERS' TALES

# shitting pretty

★
★ ★

## how to stay clean
## and healthy while traveling

TRAVELERS' TALES

# shitting pretty

*   *
 *

## how to stay clean
## and healthy while traveling

### DR. JANE WILSON-HOWARTH

TRAVELERS' TALES
SAN FRANCISCO, CALIFORNIA

Travelers' Tales and Travelers' Tales Guides are trademarks of Travelers'
Tales, Inc., 330 Townsend Street, Suite 208, San Francisco, California 94107.
www.travelerstales.com

Credits and copyright notices are given starting on page 147.

*Jacket Design: Michele Wetherbee*
*Interior Design: Kathryn Heflin and Susan Bailey*
*Illustrations: Amy Crehore*
*Page Layout: Patty Holden, using the fonts Berkeley, Copperplate, Savoye, and Birch*

Distributed by: Publishers Group West, 1700 Fourth Street, Berkeley, CA 94710.

Library of Congress Cataloging-in-Publication Data

Wilson-Howard, Jane.
    Shitting pretty : how to stay clean and healthy while traveling / by Jane Wilson-Howarth.
        p. cm.
        ISBN 1-885211-47-3 (alk. paper)
        1. Travel-Health aspects. I. Title.

        RA783.5 .W555 2000
        613.6'8–dc21                                 00-023417

First Printing

Printed in the United States of America

10 9 8 7 6 5 4 3 2

*By our bad habits we spoil our sacred river banks and furnish excellent breeding grounds for flies. A small spade is the means of salvation from a great nuisance. Leaving night-soil, cleaning the nose, or spitting on the road is a sin against God as well as humanity, and betrays a sad want of consideration for others. The man who does not cover his waste deserves a heavy penalty even if he lives in a forest.*

— MOHANDAS K. GANDHI

# TABLE OF CONTENTS

This book is meant principally as a guide to avoiding illness and it is not a substitute for a doctor's advice on your particular symptoms or situation. If you are ill, it is always wise to seek a medical consultation if you can, and avoid self-prescribing if at all possible.

# INTRODUCTION

Fayre Cloacina, goddess of this playce
Dayli resorte of all ye human race
Graciouslie grant my offerings may flow
Nor rudelie swifte not obstinatlie slow.

—*Sir John Harington*

———

Travel is a joy, full of surprises and delightful new experiences. Perhaps some of the most enjoyable times are those where one comes close to some disaster; the risks add spice, and make for great stories when you are safely back home again. But what are the risks and what is predictable in travel? Wherever you are, you'll be eating daily and needing to go to the bathroom…but will you be able to identify the necessary "facilities?" And will the commonest of travelers' ills have you needing the bathroom rather too often? This little book will—I trust—allow you to enjoy your adventures with the minimum of forced gastrointestinal stops. Within these pages you will find strategies to avoid illness and ensure a healthy trip, if you wish. Exotic eating is a delight of travel, and I offer information to allow you to judge the risk of eating any particular food so that you can decide whether you want to live (relatively) dangerously.

The last time I was memorably ill with travelers' diarrhea was when I broke my own rules. I was out in the tourist quarter of Kathmandu. I didn't feel like eating in the busiest, most popular restaurants and picked one on the edge of Thamel. Inside, it was pretentiously decorated but deserted, and I wondered why I was going to eat in a deserted restaurant: their food was likely to be stale and perhaps there was a reason for its unpopularity. I chose a Mexican meat dish, served on lettuce, garnished with cold (probably unpasteurized) sour cream and raw chopped tomatoes. I awoke in the small hours knowing I was about to be very, very ill, and lay awake most of the rest of the night waiting for the vomiting to start. I ignored my own rules, enjoyed the meal, and paid for it, albeit for a mere twenty-four hours. However much you know about avoiding traveler's diarrhea, you may—out of adventurousness or good manners—accept food you would rather have avoided.

I have worked as a health advisor and clinician in remote parts of Asia for eleven years, and on many of my trips into inaccessible orthodox communities I have been treated as an "honorary man." I am often offered delicacies. Asian men think that I am being paid a compliment, and celebrity treatment certainly facilitates my work. I am regarded as probably having an intellect equaling a man yet I am allowed to talk to the women in the community even if they are kept in purdah. But the biggest recurring prob-

I was fifteen in the Casablanca airport with a full bladder. The toilets were obvious from their smell but the sign distinguishing Gents from Ladies was in Arabic. I entered the nearest to . be confronted by indignant men using urinals. In my haste, I headed for the nearest cubicle. Once inside and my bladder empty, I realized what I'd done: I could hear the angry men outside shouting at me and dared not come out. Eventually a policeman escorted me to safety.

◆

*Dr. Jocelyne Hughes, 38, lecturer in environmental conservation, University of Oxford, UK*

lem I have in my honorary manhood is finding an acceptable place to empty my bladder. One thing I do early in any assignment is to find out how to ask to go to the bathroom in a language most local women will understand—and often this is not even the national language. Late in 1992, my work took me to refugee camps in southern Bangladesh where I met many Muslims who had fled from the terror of the regime in Myanmar. What were the refugees' health concerns? One woman spoke for many: "When we first came, conditions were dreadful. There were no latrines, and we had to walk for miles before we could relieve ourselves without anyone seeing. Mostly we tried to wait and go at night. We got all sorts of bladder symptoms from hanging on too long, but now there are latrines, things are much better." It is not only Western travelers who have problems finding somewhere to "go."

One of the curious questions I am sometimes asked is what it is like being a woman in a war zone. Admittedly being the only woman in the front line in a unit of 2,000 men in the Gulf brought one or two problems. I could write a book for the British Army on the subject of "Going to the Loo in Saudi Arabia," in a flat desert with no bushes or trees. But in other less exotic areas, such as Bosnia, Chechnya, or Nagorno-Karabakh, the question seems to imply that there are no other women in the region at all.

♦

*Kate Adie, OBE, BBC war correspondent,* Medicine Conflict and Survival (1999)

There is enormous scope for confusion and embarrassment when talking about the loo, even in your native tongue.

"My BMs are loose!" I could tell from her expression that this thin pale little girl was divulging some delicate confidence.

"Pardon?"

"My BMs are loose!"

"What are BMs?" I hadn't a clue. Brits don't know that BMs are bowel movements, but when I *did* find out, how embarrassed we both were! She was a shy ten-year-old at summer camp in Connecticut and I was an ignorant, inhibited twenty-year-old Britisher not yet fluent in the local language. I was in a foreign country, without my parents and this was my first experience of discussing unmentionable things with foreigners. Until then I had thought that only the English were truly obsessed with their bowels. Americans, it seemed, were interested, too, yet very coy, but there is an enormous vocabulary surrounding these embarrassing bodily functions.

How does one talk about one's bowel and bladder needs? How do you ask politely about the facilities? In Australia it's the "dunny" and each English public school has its own euphemism: at Winchester it's "the forakers," Lancing "the groves," Felstead "the shants," Leys "the Styx," Westminster "the japs," and at Malborough they go "to the woods." English vocabulary is rich. I might say that I'd like to visit the jakes; use the cloakroom; rest room; bathroom; lavatory; WC; privy; latrine; thunder box; john; karzi; bog; crapper; dike; roundhouse; the smallest room; the wee room; the necessary room;

Mr. Johnson and I walked arm-in-arm up the High Street to my house in James's Court; it was a dusky night; I could not prevent his being assailed by the evening effluvia of Edinburgh...walking the streets of Edinburgh at night was pretty perilous and a good deal odoriferous. The peril is much abated by the enforce[ment of] the city laws against throwing foul water from the windows, but...there being no covered sewers, the odour still continues.

◆

*James Boswell, Scottish biographer of Samuel Johnson (1773)*

garderobe; the house where the emperor goes on foot; the honeypot; the thinking house; the throne room; powder my nose; pick a daisy; have a poo; be excused; spend a penny; have a Jimmy Riddle; shake the dew off the lily; wash my hands; view the plumbing; go and see a man about a dog (or a horse); take a dump; go to pinch off a loaf; got a bull in the chute; shake hands with an old friend; have a slash; splash my boots; go to the loo. Loo is said to come from the "*Gardez l'eau*" (Watch out for water) that medieval citizens cried before emptying their "pysse pottes" into the street from an upstairs window.

We haven't always been so coy; from the Middle Ages until the Victorian era, European royalty gave audiences in the garderobe, while the sovereign sat upon a "great stool of ease." Many Asians too are happy to talk explicitly. As a more experienced traveler, I was sitting through a long village health meeting in Lombok, Indonesia, and my bladder was getting

On a night train to Harare, I entered the toilet to find the light wasn't working. Returned to my seat, found my headlight, entered the toilet again, locked the door, went to sit down, and looked up into the eyes of a local holding the lightbulb. He was traveling without a ticket, hoping that he could hide in the dark undetected.

♦

*Dr. Anne Denning, 37, ophthalmic surgeon, Bournemouth, UK*

Closed the door of the windowless Parisian toilet. Pitch black inside. Felt for the light switch. There wasn't one. Came out. Looked for the switch outside. There wasn't one. Went back in. Still pitch-black. Still no switch. Getting desperate. Try anyway. Lock the door. Light goes on. *Mon Dieu!* Door lock is also the light switch!

♦

*David White, 65, retired headmaster, Ayrshire, Scotland*

fuller and fuller. Finally I had to ask. I leaned across to a female colleague and asked, "Where is the *kamar kecil* [small room]?"

"Do you need to throw away big water [have a shit] or small water [a wee]?"

I had been in the country some months but was still embarrassed by Indonesian directness. I didn't want to discuss my toilet needs, but when I said "Only small water" she took me to a bathing place with a minute drain hole in the corner of the concrete construction. I stood looking baffled.

"Just go there!" And she stood waiting and watching me.

"Umm…"

"Just go there!" she said pointing again.

In my embarrassment, my command of Indonesian left me, and I couldn't think how to say that I wanted to be alone. I weed hurriedly, pulled up my underwear, and fled, blushing. She stood there dumbfounded. "Don't you need to wash?" There: my filthy foreign habits were revealed.

The shared experiences within this book should help future travelers avoid embarrassment when needing to bathe or use the lavatory. This book will also help reduce the amount of times readers will need to go to the bathroom: within these pages you will find the pearls of wisdom that will enable you to sidestep travelers' diarrhea, that oh-so-common of travelers' afflictions. So read on, and "go" in peace.

The Amazon city of Porto Velho has little space to reflect, so I sat on the toilet to read. A leaflet-bearing hand and then a face appeared encouraging me to open my heart to God. The Lord does work in mysterious ways.

◆

*Peter Hutchison, 32, author,* Bradt Guide to the Amazon, *London, UK*

# Chapter 1

## TRAVELERS' DIARRHEA
### KNOWING IT, AVOIDING IT

The young American put his head down to the milk-bowl and the
milk darkened, from white to grey, as his head blocked out the light.
The bowl was half a calabash. He held it in his palms and felt the
warmth coming through. There were black hairs floating on the
surface and a faint smell of pitch. He tilted the bowl till the froth
brushed against his moustache. "Shall I?" He paused before his
lips touched the milk. Then he tilted it again and gulped.

— *Bruce Chatwin,* Anatomy of Restlessness

---

*T*raveling is a little hazardous; that is what makes it
exciting. But what are the risks? What about all those
tropical diseases that are out to get you: plague, hantavirus, dengue, rabies, cholera, typhoid, typhus (what's the
difference?), tuberculosis, dysentery, yellow fever, malaria?
Malaria literally means bad air, the name originating from a
time when the disease was rampant in Europe and people got it
from venturing into dank, marshy places. No one understood
how it was caught; it was a mysterious and feared infection. A
lot of worries about this and other travelers' ills stem from mis-
understanding or ignorance of avoidance strategies, so read on
and see how risks can be minimized.

It surprises many people that it is not tropical disease that
takes most travelers' lives. It is accidents that are most likely to
kill you. Infectious or communicable diseases take surprisingly
few adventurers' lives: less than 1 percent of those few who do
die abroad. Tropical infections don't kill many travelers, but that

1

doesn't mean that we avoid illness: on the contrary, most of us get sick when we travel. The most common infection which gets us is diarrhea, and studies say that about half of those traveling to the developing world will get a dose of Montezuma's revenge each trip. The highest-risk destinations are tropical Latin America and the Indian subcontinent; North Americans import their diarrhea and dysentery from Mexico, Ecuador, Peru, and Bolivia, and Europeans bring theirs mostly from India and Nepal. It isn't just travelers who suffer either; the diarrheal diseases cause a lot of illness (and even deaths) in the local population, too. You only need to look at the consistency of the brown deposits on the streets of Kathmandu to realize this.

What is travelers' diarrhea? Diarrhea means loosening of the bowels so that the sufferer "goes" at least three times in twenty-four hours. The most common form makes you ill for around thirty-six hours then symptoms disappear without doing any real harm, except perhaps leaving a somewhat battle-worn tail end. There are as many names for travelers' diarrhea as there are kinds of microbes that cause it. There is gastroenteritis, food poisoning, upset stomach, Montezuma's revenge (from South America), gyppy tummy (from Egypt), Delhi belly, the Kathmandu quickstep, Tandoori trots (from the subcontinent), the Aztec two-step, turista, the runs, the squits, the squirts, the

Although we traveled for over a year in Latin America neither my husband nor I became ill with "the trots." We were not overcautious about sampling local foods, but made sure we ate only food that was served piping hot. We ate street food, but only dishes that were cooked as we waited. We stuck to bottled water in most places.

♦

*Karen Birch, 36, sales coordinator, Sussex, UK*

2

screaming shits.... The most common culprit is snappily known as enterotoxigenic *Escherichia coli* or ETEC to those who know it more intimately. These little blighters produce a toxin that acts in the same way as cholera, stimulating an outpouring of water and salts into the bowel; the result is thirty-six to forty-eight hours of frequent trips to the lavatory to deposit said water and salts. Studies have shown that this is responsible for up to 40 percent of cases of traveler's diarrhea, and this is the most likely criminal especially in Africa and Central and South America. ETEC is the most common but there are others.

- Among ETEC's many cousins are: Enteroadherent, entero-hemorrhagic E.coli, and others

- Rotaviruses or "small round viruses"

- *Campylobacter*, causing gripping pains with the diarrhea

- *Shigella*—only ten bacteria need to get in for a brisk bout of bacilliary dysentery (see Chapter 9)

- Other bacterial causes of diarrhea, like *Salmonella* food poisoning

- *Giardia*, which will cause you to generate smelly emissions that will make you most unpopular

- A variety of other parasites and worms (see Chapter 11)

- Amebic dysentery

- *Cryptosporidium*, which causes a tedious type of diarrhea that lasts for two weeks with a lot of cramps; there is no specific treatment

- Norwalk and a catalog of rarer diarrhea-causing viruses

- Cholera

- *Cyclospora*

- Tropical infections (like malaria) which can cause diarrhea along with other symptoms.

There is a range of nontropical, noninfectious causes of diarrhea that are unrelated to travel but may occur in travelers coincidentally. Just because you are traveling and you have diarrhea does not mean that you have travelers' diarrhea. See a doctor if in doubt.

The microbes responsible for causing stomach problems abroad are many and varied, yet fortunately for us the prevention strategies and the treatments are similar for most of these. So where does it come from? Most "stomach upsets" in travelers come via a revolting route known by medics as fecal-oral transmission; I call it the filth-to-mouth route, or getting someone else's feces in your mouth. Someone has the Kathmandu quickstep and uses the long-drop lavatory but doesn't wash his hands before preparing your sandwich and soon you too are running to the loo. Most travelers' diarrhea reaches your mouth via contaminated food: food handled by someone with traces of feces on their hands. The term diarrhea includes the full range of filth-to-mouth infections listed above (the exotic ones are detailed in

> ── ★ ★ ──
>
> In the 1970s, Goa offered few tourist facilities. The toilet was a stone cubicle with two breeze blocks to keep the feet above ground level. The area between the blocks was puzzlingly clean. One day though, while I was squatting to empty my bowels, a small pig appeared and vacuumed up everything I'd produced. My dilemma was then whether to continue to tempt fate by eating those delicious local sausages.
>
> ◆
>
> *Jane Thakker, 46, sail-training coordinator, Warsash, Hampshire, UK*

Chapter 8), but in addition there are filth-to-mouth diseases (including typhoid, paratyphoid, hepatitis A and E, and some of the worm infestations), which cause symptoms other than diarrhea. All the microbes in this formidable list can be avoided by following similar, simple precautions.

None of these microbes survives cooking. However filthy the food was when it arrived in the kitchen and however unhygienic the cook has been, as long as the food has been thoroughly cooked it will not harm you. Well-cooked, steaming hot food is safe, but food that is lukewarm or has been cooked, allowed to go cold, and then is handled by someone is risky. Cold dishes like quiche, pizza, and savory pies might be a source of Delhi belly if the food has been badly stored or handled with dirty hands. Meat is more risky than vegetarian dishes, because animals can become infected while they are still alive, and, once slaughtered, flesh is a better environment for the survival and multiplication of harmful microbes than is vegetable matter.

Salads are often grown in highly contaminated ground (people without toilets often relieve themselves in vegetable gardens), and low-growing fruits, especially strawberries, can easily become contaminated by human feces. The most hazardous raw foods are those that can trap filth in crevices and are difficult to clean—lettuce is among the worst. Conversely, smooth-skinned items can be cleaned quite well, so carefully washed tomatoes and items that can be peeled like carrots or radishes are fairly safe. Washing or peeling is also advisable to reduce the amount of pesticides you swallow. There are no foods that are 100 percent safe, but the challenge is to reduce risks to a minimum, without making the traveling experience one of precautions, worries, and anxieties from morning until night.

There are innumerable myths about what causes bad stomachs in travelers, but it is nearly always contaminated food, or occasionally—just occasionally—dirty water. Mellor's *voice of experience* (this page) illustrates some of the common misconceptions of many travelers. The myth of locals being immune is ill-informed travelers' folklore, and the distressingly common idea that eating bad food will immunize you is responsible for a lot of unnecessary illness in travelers, as well as exposing them to dangerous filth-to-mouth infections like typhoid. In short, hot street food = safe. Hotel water = may be safe, could be chancy. Ice cream in India or Nepal = clench your buttocks.

I drink the water provided by hotels abroad, eat on the street, and indulge in ice cream on a hot day. I believe that the introduction of a few foreign microbes into one's system assists acclimatization; if locals can eat ice cream without suffering dire consequences, so can I. I have suffered an attack of dysentery in India which rendered me fearful of relaxing clenched buttocks, and been laid low by a bug that debilitated me for the entire overland journey to Lhasa. Both were contracted in supposedly safe environments.

♦

T. Mellor, Middlesex, UK,
Letter in Wanderlust (1998)

## *Tips*

➤ Peel it, boil it, cook it, or forget it: this is the maxim to protect you from travelers' diarrhea and other fecal-oral diseases when visiting less sanitary places.

➤ In the Middle East and South Asia, some melon sellers puncture the fruits and soak them in roadside drains to make them weigh heavy before sale. This is a probable explanation of why, in the days of the British Raj, melons were blamed for Indian chlolera outbreaks.

➢ Choose freshly cooked, piping hot food rather than reheated food or food kept lukewarm on a hotel buffet.

➢ Sizzling hot street food is likely to be safer than just-warm food, even if produced by an international hotel.

➢ In international hotels order à la carte foods if you can.

➢ In busy local restaurants eat what everyone else is eating; don't ask for dishes that are "exotic" for them.

➢ Avoid salads—especially lettuce—and also unclean-able soft fruits like strawberries unless these items have been grown and prepared hygienically. In Kathmandu, La Paz, and many other places, the only safe lettuce is boiled lettuce.

As I was keeping my balance over the hole in the outhouse in Gansu province (China,) I became aware of a movement below. Something was wallowing in the sludge; it had a snout and two eyes. There was a pig living in the toilet pit, guzzling the day's delivery.

◆

*Sam Cowan, 27, travel-mad journalist, Ilford, Essex, UK*

In a snack bar in Arusha, Tanzania, the deep-fried chicken was so hot that I had to hold it with paper serviettes. Yet as I ate, I discovered, too late, ice along the still frozen central bone. Driving along about twelve hours later, the salmonella hit me, and before I had a chance to pull over I emptied my stomach and bowel, and the evacuation continued in hospital for three days. Now I cut into my finger food and look at it before I eat.

◆

*Steve Foreman, 47, explorer, Walesby, Nottinghamshire, UK*

➤ Fresh mayonnaise can carry *Salmonella* bacteria.

➤ Dishes containing meat are riskier than vegetarian foods so becoming vegetarian when you travel will reduce stomach troubles.

➤ Fried rice often makes people ill in Nepal, especially if it is made with leftover meat. The ingredients have often been hanging around unrefrigerated and are often flash-fried and thus inadequately reheated.

➤ Where environmental hygiene is poor, pork and dog are the riskiest of meat types. Pigs and dogs are often the local rubbish disposal consultants. Any pork (or dog) that you choose to eat must be very thoroughly cooked. Nepalis say that it is unwise to eat pork during the hot season—for good reason.

---
★
★ ★
---

A market town in Hunan, China, boasted a hotel so grand that the latrines were indoors, on the second floor. Crouching over a drafty hole, I was alarmed to hear voices coming from beneath me. Imagine hearing voices coming from a lavatory bowl, you'll know how vulnerable I felt. I looked down. There in the room below was a thirty-foot-wide pool full of what came through the holes above; on the shores of this indescribable sea stood The Three Most Unfortunate Men in the World, ladling out fertilizer for the veggies. Salad is not a wise choice in China.

◆

*Catherine Hopper, 37, cycling Buddhist, Manchester, UK*

➤ In most developing countries, fresh milk—even milk that says it is pasteurized—should be boiled before drinking.

➤ Yogurt is usually safe because the milk is boiled before fermentation and the final product is slightly acidic and thus less favorable for the survival of noxious bacteria.

➤ Sorbet tends to be acidic and, since acids are unfavorable to bacteria, this is a fairly safe food.

➤ Ice cream is often risky in developing countries since power cuts make it difficult to store safely.

➤ Ice, too, is often made with dirty water or handled with dirty hands. Sometimes it is delivered in huge blocks that are dumped onto the ground outside the drinks stall or hotel.

➤ There are a few enormously rare tropical infections that come via the filth-to-mouth route. These are hantavirus, which comes from eating foods that have been excreted upon or nibbled by mice; Weil's disease (leptospirosis), from swallowing food or drink contaminated with rat urine; and Lassa fever, which often comes from consuming food contaminated with the urine of the multimammate rat. Following two simple rules reduces the risk of acquiring all of these nasty but rare infections: eat your food piping hot, and drink safe water.

In Arambol, a one-tap fishing village in Goa, I came down with extremely bad diarrhea. Innumerable toilet visits had me teetering on two rocks sheltered by palm leaves; the balancing act was made more precarious by charging hungry pigs.

♦

*Vincent Ward, 39, reluctant farmhand, Chiba-ken, Japan*

# Chapter 2

## WHAT'S IN THE WATER?
### WHEN IS IT SAFE TO DRINK?

A POOEM

Hanging latrines can be fun
Everyone loves a shit in the sun.
Over fields, crops and lakes
We drop our curly little cakes.

And thus we spread so much disease
Without a thought, with consummate ease.
Worms, amoebae, parasites and cysts
Destined all for deadly trysts.

Spread by dogs, children and chickens
Provides–guaranteed–all that sickens.
Into our tummies they quickly go
For the rumbling diarrhea show.

So all tasty fruit please do peel,
Or your fate you will seal.
Eat nothing but hot cooked food
Then your health will stay fair rude.

—*Derrick Ikin, 53,* poet laureate of the defecatorium, Maputo, Mozambique

———

*M*ost travelers seem preoccupied with water quality, unaware that it is bad food hygiene that most often makes them sick. Perhaps one reason for this misapprehension is that there is a lot of investment in clean water and there is money to be made from selling water purification devices to travelers. There *are* outbreaks of water-borne illnesses—especially during times of civil unrest, war, disaster, and chaos—but the vast majority of travelers' intestinal symptoms are due to poor food-handling practices. The reason is that contaminated hands can carry millions of harmful microbes, which can then be inoculated into food, breed to produce millions more microbes, and thus produce a very effective "infective dose" of harmful bacteria. Conversely, germs that enter clean-looking drinking water may die for want of food or may become so dispersed and diluted that when that slightly contaminated water is swallowed, only one or two bacteria enter the body and these may be in insufficient numbers to cause illness. I am not suggesting that it is wise to drink any water anywhere, but that drinking pure water will not completely protect you.

And even in Third World countries the quality of domestic water is a lot better than it used to be, and many international hotels ensure that their water supply is clean. Ask if you are unsure. Studies in several Asian countries suggest that bottled water produced locally may not be entirely safe. Most of it is not even "mineral water" but treated (or untreated) tap water. Yet there has been a boom in "mineral water" production so that it is available in a surprising

Corrie insisted that if the locals in Cairo could drink the water, so could she. She was hit with a severe case of the runs—the original "gyppy" tummy—and eventually sought medical advice. Despite treatment with vitamins and constipation pills in Egypt, she was still ill a month after returning home.

♦

*Jo Surtees, 29,*
*wandering English teacher,*
*Iwate-Ken, Japan*

number of quite remote destinations now. The quality is patchy, but if I need water in a city in the developing world, I drink bottled water. It is usually safe enough. Other kinds of bottled drinks, the colas and other carbonated drinks, should be safe because the contents are somewhat acidic which is unfavorable for microbes, and boxed drinks will also be safe. Beware of "homemade" drinks that have involved a lot of handling during concoction.

If you need really safe water—you may be traveling with a young baby or your own health dictates that you must take special care—the safest means of treating water is to boil it. Water that has been brought to a good rolling boil is safe, and even water heated above 140°F/60°C is unlikely to harbor any nasty microbes. When I was traveling in the remote mountains of Nepal with my three-month-old, I carried a metal vacuum flask. Whenever we stopped to eat, or we stopped at a tea shop, I asked for the flask to be filled with boiling water. Kept hot like this for fifteen minutes or so, even water that has not been properly boiled will be ultrasafe. Another precaution: very sensitive stom-

I sterilize all drinking water with tincture of iodine. This is extremely cheap, and it is also widely available (from pharmacists), although you need to check the strength. I use five to ten drops per liter of the English variety, though rarely use more than six or seven unless the water is particularly suspect. I let it stand for twenty minutes before drinking. Although the bottle says for external use only, it is safe if used in this way, and has kept me healthy on many extended trips where pure water is hard to find. A vial of iodine is much lighter than a water filter (backpackers must consider weight). One drawback is the horrible taste, which I counteract with powdered drink: added in small quantities, it just takes the taste of the iodine away without making the water too sweet.

♦

*Phil Brabbs, 42, teacher trainer, Plzen, Czech Republic*

achs may protest if there is a lot of sediment in the water, and turbid water makes chemical sterilization methods less effective. Leave very turbid water to stand or filter it.

After boiling, the next best way of treating water is chemically. Chemical "sterilization" takes time (thirty minutes), gives water a taste, and does not kill all microbes. But for most purposes the water will be rendered safe enough. Safest of the chemical options is iodine, and chlorine is the next most efficient means. Silver products are the least purifying—although these have the longest shelf life so are good for the occasional traveler. For travel to regions where environmental hygiene standards are very poor, I use iodine if boiling is impossible.

Alcohol is a poison. Even in its purest, Highland malt form, it is toxic, but when its origin is some still in a shack, it is likely to contain unpredictable levels of additional poisons. Be ready to face the consequences if you drink too much. Beware of spirits; distilled drinks can contain extremely dangerous toxic methanol that can cause permanent blindness. Undistilled drinks of lower alcoholic content (less than 40 percent) are unsafe if (as they usually are) they are prepared with dirty water (e.g. Tibetan *chang*). An exception is Nepali *toongba*,

One hot day in Jaipur, India, I decided to try a long lemon-yellow sherbet drink that a man was selling from a rickety stall on bicycle wheels. It was ice cold and delicious, but I soon realized this was no ordinary lemonade. The bhang [cannabis] made me drunk fast and then I was hit by dramatic diarrhea that had me loitering close to the loo for the next twelve hours. Next day I was exhausted but the diarrhea had abated. In the future I would be wary of cocktails and messed-about-with drinks.

♦

*Simon Howarth, 45,*
*civil engineer, Cambridge, UK*

where boiling water is poured over fermented millet, but make sure that the water is boiling and the pot preheated. In Pakistan, one brewery is rumored to put glycerol in as a preservative for beer that is sent far from the hill station near Rawalpindi where it is produced. Anyone consuming more than one bottle suffers mild diarrhea.

## *Tips*

> The newer you are to tropical travel the more careful you should be about what you eat and drink.

> It is not necessary to boil water for twenty minutes as recommended in many guides; this merely wastes fuel. Water that has been brought to the boil is safe enough, and boiling remains the best method of making contaminated water safe.

> Failing this, add an iodine-based water purification tablet or drops to the bottled water and leave for the recommended period before drinking.

> Adding vitamin C can reduce the unpleasant taste

"I eat and drink everything," said a green young volunteer on his first assignment to Bangladesh. Six months later an even greener young man was medically evacuated to Bangkok suffering from dehydration and blood loss. Hanging latrines, although illegal, are still found in rural and urban areas of Bangladesh. These makeshift bamboo pole and woven wall constructions allow the user to squat over water or rice fields and defecate, thus contaminating water and allowing dogs and chickens easy access to fecal meals. Children playing with puppies, and chickens eating scraps, share diseases from these hanging health horrors.

◆

*Derrick Ikin, 53, Swiss development consultant, Maputo, Mozambique*

from iodine, but this must not be added until the purifying thirty minutes has been completed.

➤ Bottled water is almost certainly safer than any alternative local supply, which has not been treated, but it is not a guarantee of trouble-free travels.

➤ In the West, bottled water is untreated spring water from a safe source, whereas in the developing world it is often treated tap water and so should not strictly be called "mineral water."

➤ International hotels will provide you with safe drinking water if you ask.

➤ When staying in a more down-market place ask for a glass of boiling water. If it is hot, you know it is safe enough. In Indonesia, eating houses offer *air putih*. This is boiled water that is often served still warm; it is safe but beware of added ice which may be contaminated.

> My new Brazilian boyfriend and I, on an Amazon boat journey, arrived in Alter do Chão, a place of extraordinary beauty. We saw a little of it before a violent bout of diarrhea kicked in. I spent the next few hours being propped up on the toilet by him, both of us close to passing out! Naturally, I later married that man who was so willing and able!
>
> ◆
>
> *Susanne Padilha, 38, Brazilophile, Hong Kong*

➤ If you are offered a drink—or food—which you think may be contaminated, take as little as possible; the less you consume, the less you risk stomach trouble.

Travelers in developing countries can be lulled into a false sense of security by assuming that bottled water is safe water. Tests and visits to bottling plants in Nepal showed that while the majority of samples were free of fecal contamination, some rogue companies were merely bottling inadequately treated tap water. Quality control is a major issue—even leading companies lack on-site lab facilities to test for many impurities. A number rely on one-off tests in Europe at the start of production to accredit their brands. Nepal, like many countries with limited resources, has very few regulations in place to protect the quality of bottled water. This problem is not restricted to the developing world. In the USA, the Natural Resources Defense Council (1999) tested 1,000 samples of 103 U.S. brands and found that at least one-third had levels of bacteria and chemicals that exceeded the standards regulating the bottled water industry.

◆

*Greg Whiteside, 41, water engineer, WaterAid, Nepal*

# Chapter 3

## EATING RIGHT
### THE PLEASURES AND
### PERILS OF SEAFOOD

Eat Fish—Live Longer
Eat Oysters—Love Longer
Eat Clams—Last Longer

— *Bumper sticker, Delaware*

———

*T*here is good medical evidence that eating at least one portion of oily fish each week helps prevent atherosclerosis and consequent heart disease; fish and shellfish form part of a healthy diet when you are staying at home, but on your travels, you may need to be cautious about foods that have been harvested from the sea, rivers, or even rice fields; they can be risky. In less-developed Asian countries people use "hanging latrines" that allow feces to fall into rice fields or fish ponds, so recycling parasites and filth-to-mouth microbes. Many edible water creatures feed by filtration and so accumulate and concentrate harmful microbes. And seawater does not kill microbes so that in Peru, for example, delicious ceviche (marinated raw sea fish) was identified as a source of cholera.

In the 1960s the people of the Philippine island of Luzon started to develop a mysterious wasting disease that caused prolonged and debilitating diarrhea. The epidemic was finally blamed on *Capillaria* worms that live in shrimps, fish, and birds, as well as in people. Locals loved eating "jumping salad" (made from shrimps so fresh they were still moving) and other raw delicacies: snails, crabs, squid, and the vital organs of fish, goats, and cows. The disease—once diagnosed—was treatable, but could have been avoided in the first place by cooking the food. Improved disposal of excreta reduced the number of people suffering from these parasites.

Undercooked seafood is risky all over the world. Even pickled raw fish from California or the Netherlands can be a source of herring worms, although these cause—at most—a transient touch of nausea and a few stomach cramps. And cases of paralytic shellfish poisoning are even recorded occasionally from the chilly waters around Britain. Symptoms begin (typically within three hours of eating shellfish) with tingling around the mouth and throat, dizziness, and a floating sensation. There can also be headache, nausea, and vomiting. The tingling and numbness progresses, and the muscles become affected so that breathing may stop altogether. In Britain, mussels eaten during the summer are usually the culprits.

> ★
> ── ★ ★ ──
>
> When the mood is right there's nothing better than a meal of sushi, which of course is raw fish with rice and other garnishes. Any good restaurant worth its reputation will serve only the highest quality ingredients prepared to eliminate all worms and parasites. If you're worried about safety, be sure to go only to restaurants that do a brisk business. That way you'll be certain all the fish is fresh.
>
> ◆
>
> *Larry Habegger, 47,*
> *writer and editor,*
> *San Francisco, California*

From time to time in tropical seas there are dramatic blooms of tiny dinoflagellate animals that make the water look red: so-called red tides. This danger is signaled by the deaths of large numbers of fish and sea birds. It is most common along polluted coasts. Local fishermen usually know not to catch fish during these red tides since they are poisonous. Filter-feeding shellfish concentrate the red tide poisons and so must also be avoided at these times. If you must eat fish, choose individuals with clear eyes, a firm intact body that smells all right. Symptoms develop within half an hour of eating contaminated fish and may progress to fatal paralysis in twelve hours.

Ciguatera fish poisoning is more difficult to recognize; it happens when there is no obvious change in the sea. It causes several deaths a year worldwide. Like red tide poisoning, it is also due to fish accumulating dinoflagellate toxins from their food. The liver, viscera, and sexual organs or roe of large and also scaleless warm-water shore or reef fish are most likely to contain the toxin. Moray eels should not be eaten because of the high risk of ciguatera poisoning. An early sign that a fish is affected is that as you are eating you may notice tingling or numbness of the mouth, and this progresses to vomiting, diarrhea, and cramps. Some people are left with a weird, fairly long-term change in temperature sensation when cold objects feel burning hot and painful to touch. This settles with time.

Scombrotoxic poisoning occurs when the red flesh of tuna, mackerel and their relatives (including albacore, skipjack, and bonito), and the flesh of tinned fish such as sardines and anchovies, or others including mahimahi, blue fish, amberjack, and herring are decomposed by bacteria to produce histamine poisons. These toxins often cause a tingling or smarting sensation in the mouth, or a peppery or bitter taste in the fish. If you do not stop eating at this point, you will go on to experience flushing, sweating, itching, abdominal pain, vomiting, and dizziness which usually goes away within twenty-four hours. This kind of poisoning is avoided by eating fresh fish or by removing the guts and freezing fish as soon as possible after being caught. The problem is most common in hot climates, because decomposition begins so quickly. Medical treatment is not necessary.

# $\mathcal{T}ips$

➤ In Southeast Asia, lightly cooked shellfish and sea fish can be sources of exotic parasites.

➤ If fish or shellfish may have been taken from contaminated waters, ensure that it is well cooked. For seafood from a contaminated environment to be really safe it should be boiled for ten minutes or steamed for thirty.

➤ It is dangerous to eat fish or shellfish caught during red tides; be wary of eating fish from polluted seas. When buying fresh fish, check to see that it looks and smells fresh.

➤ Even in temperate climates be wary of mollusks. Eating mussels that stay closed after cooking is likely to make you ill.

➤ Avoid eating very large reef fish; these may come with special ciguatera poisons.

➤ Puffer fish or *fugu*, beloved of the Japanese, is said to be outstandingly delicious but if improperly prepared is

The mutton fish, or *pawa*, although resembling india rubber in toughness and color, is very excellent and substantial food for explorers, both European and native…[but] the sea anemone…is the most extraordinary food that ever afforded nutriment to the human body, and…in eating it, the eyes should be kept closely shut.

◆

*Charles Heaphy, VC, 1820–1881, English-born New Zealander, painter, surveyor, and explorer*

lethal. There are other fish that may also be toxic in Southeast Asia and the Indo-Pacific, so get a local cook to prepare fish for you.

➤ Strangely shaped or very colorful fish are more likely to harbor ciguatera toxin than dull fish-shaped fish.

➤ During the mating season, horseshoe crabs become poisonous; don't eat them.

➤ The sexual and other internal organs of a wide variety of sea creatures can be poisonous; it is best to eat only the flesh. And eat your sea cucumbers and fish peeled or skinned.

I awoke feeling nauseated after a particularly rich meal of butterfish in southern Africa. Then I vomited and began to develop a fever. The illness I had first thought was simple food poisoning turned out to be cerebral malaria, but I don't think I'll be able to look a butterfish in the eye again.

◆

*Barbara Ikin, 47, development worker, Mozambique*

---

The delight of trips to Brittany (Bretagne) in France is the seafood. I love to buy fresh mussels or scallops and live langoustine (scampi) and cook them myself at the campsite. Seafood here is always very fresh and exceptionally tasty. The French give food a high priority so the turnover in shops and food stalls is fast, and fish and shellfish are so much fresher than you'll find in England. I think that the best seafood comes from temperate waters. The much-praised barramunda lungfish of Australia and prawns raised in the tropics cannot be compared to the seafood of Brittany.

◆

*Arnold Thomas, 67, chef, Ewell, Surrey, UK*

# Chapter 4

## WEIRD FOODS
### THE RISKS OF FEARLESS DINING

Dr. Buckland [popular and respected visitor to the London Zoo]
used to say that he had eaten his way straight through the whole
animal creation, and that the worst thing was the mole—that
was utterly horrible…there is one thing even worse than
a mole, and that was a blue-bottle fly.

— *Augustus J. C. Hare,* The Story of My Life ( *1882)*

---

*I* was walking through some rice fields in rural Thailand with a local engineer when a slender green snake shot across the path just ahead of us. Interested in my friend's lack of reaction to the animal, I asked, "Was that a venomous snake?"

"No, it wasn't venomous and it is not good to eat either." In his eyes, this species was a complete write-off. Later I sat down to a delicious and diverse meal of all kinds of tasty tidbits of assorted textures and flavors. I asked about the slightly gelatinous black cubes in the stir-fry.

If you travel widely, you are going to encounter food that is unusual, strange, maybe even immoral or just plain weird. Long ago I adopted a rule for strange encounters, and it has become my motto: wherever I go, whatever people I visit, I bow to their kings, respect their gods, and eat their viands no matter what. There is *nothing* I will not eat or drink at least once. I am a culinary pagan, and I worship at every altar.

◆

*Richard Sterling,*
The Fearless Diner

"This is congealed ducks' blood," my host explained, delighted I was enjoying the food. At this point I stopped enjoying the food. Thailand is renowned for its delicious cuisine and for its amazing range of foods. Shopping in Thailand is fascinating; I find myself wondering how the weird ingredients can be prepared for the table. Who, for example, might want to nibble giant water scorpions (known also as toe-biters) that seem to be a local delicacy?

Unfortunately the foods that Thais, and many of the people of Southeast and East Asia, enjoy cause some special health problems. This is because many "delicacies" are eaten raw or undercooked, and it is this lack of cooking (rather than the weird ingredients) that causes trouble. The region is well known for its great variety of exotic parasites. There is a good range of mosquito-borne infections (two kinds of elephantiasis, dengue, malaria, etc.), and there are gnathostome worms available to those who eat fresh-

In the Bangkok emergency room I explained my symptoms to the Thai doctor. Peering into my eye, he felt for the hard lump above my right eyebrow that had become my recent traveling companion. "You have *gnathostomiasis*," he announced. "It's a worm that grows under the skin, and yours is quite big so you must have had it for some time. We'll do a blood test, but there's only a 50 percent chance that it will show positive, as it only comes up at certain times, for feeding."

"Feeding!? Feeding on what?"

"Well, it lives in your soft tissues and feeds on nutrients in your blood. The usual remedy is to surgically remove it, although if you decide not to, the average life span of these worms is only about ten years."

He went on to explain that one gets this worm from eating undercooked shellfish here in Thailand. I had expected a sinus infection. Maybe even a brain tumor. But a worm living in my head? Why did I come here?

◆

*Alison Wright, "Don't Eat the Shellfish,"* Travelers' Tales Food

water crabs, raw tadpoles, frogs, and snakes. Gnathostomiasis causes lumps under the skin. Raw freshwater fish harbor *Clonorchis* liver flukes, which can cause a rather unpleasant long-lasting illness, while raw Chinese beetles and grubs may give you worm-filled lumps in the bowel, and raw freshwater shrimps in many regions may give you angiostrongyliasis: a nasty little worm that occasionally sets up home in the brain or eyes. Yet interestingly, Indonesians are wary of some foods, especially during pregnancy: they say that pineapples cause miscarriage, squid cause obstructed difficult labor, and prawns will cause the baby to be born bottom first.

In Kenya, I've eaten locusts freshly fried in butter; they were delicious, and perfectly safe to eat. On the other hand, under-cooked giant African land snails carry the risk of angiostrongyliasis. Eating raw freshwater crabs in Nigeria and Zaire may give you worm cysts and abscesses in the neck. Avoid all these nasty parasites by eating your shrimps, beetles, and snails well cooked.

The only birds known to be poisonous are three species of pitohuis, thrushlike perching birds from Papua New Guinea. They produce a powerful toxin very similar to that of South American poison arrow frogs, so that licking the feathers makes your mouth go numb and tingly. Presumably eating their flesh would do you no good, and it is unlikely that cooking will inactivate the toxin.

Wondering what to try for supper one day in Thailand, I was intrigued by "waterfall beef" on the menu. This was meat so fresh, and raw, that the blood was dripping off in a "waterfall." It was delicious, and fortunately this cow hadn't previously dined on tapeworm.

◆

*Simon Howarth, 45*
*gastronome, Cambridge, UK*

The people of Sulawesi, Indonesia, have some odd eating

habits. The Bugis, who were traditionally pirates said to be the original bogeymen, favor offal of all sorts and especially soup made from the intestinal contents of buffalo. While this is well cooked and thus safe, I could never bring myself to try it. Dog meat is eaten in many parts of the world, but in North Sulawesi, it is actually the local delicacy—stringy street mutt cooked with lots of chilies. As long as this is well cooked and freshly cooked (i.e., hot), this dish should not carry any special health risks, although since these dogs are city scavengers, they are likely to be riddled with parasites; dogs are certainly known to carry *Giardia*. Fruit bats (also known as flying foxes) live a healthier lifestyle, are tasty, and pretty safe to eat. Most of us will consider dog meat an unenticing dish, but Antarctic explorers have been forced to eat their dogs, and at least one unfortunate succumbed to vitamin A intoxication—from eating dog liver. Polar bear liver, too, is dangerous for the same reason.

Undercooked beef, buffalo, and yak are popular dishes in many Third World countries, but if the animals have grazed where people have defecated, the meat is likely to be contaminated with beef tapeworm. One

Chinese engineering contractors, working near Beergunj in the lowlands of Nepal, were out hunting snakes after dark, scrambling around with torches, trying to dig them out of their holes to eat. Locals became alarmed, and mistaking the Chinese workers for *dacoits* (bandits), mounted an attack. The Chinese spoke no Nepali so could not explain why they were acting so suspiciously, got beaten up, and subsequently complained to the police. One way to solve the problem of rabies in Nepal is to get more Chinese contractors working in the country; they will eat all the dogs, and we will have no more rabies. Chinese eat anything!

◆

*Dinesh Shrestha, 39, civil engineer, Kathmandu, Nepal*

winter in Ladakh, India, I was offered slices of yak meat as a snack. This was completely raw and crunchy from the ice within the meat; the maximum daytime temperature was around 14°F/ -10°C. Even at subzero temperatures there is a risk of parasites: tape-, round-, and *Trichinella* worms survive in very severe weather conditions. Peoples of the high Himalaya love meat in most forms (there are few vegetables available), and one is often offered strips of dried (and sometimes smoked) beef or yak

Villagers say that the water monitor is a very useful creature. You must kill the lizard and hang it up over a pot on the cooking fire so that its fat drips out. Then all you need do is apply the merest smear of this fat to the rim of the cup of your enemy or to his plate, and he will be dead by morning— and no one will know how.

♦

*Lennie Domingo, 61, irrigation engineer, Sri Lanka*

to chew with your drinks. I don't think these are altogether safe either. In warmer climates, armadillo tacos in Mexico and the Southwest U.S. have been blamed in some cases of leprosy in travelers. These animals undoubtedly are prone to leprosy but a little cooking will destroy the bacteria. Eat your armadillos well done too, or stick to beans.

It can be tempting, especially when camping in a remote place, to go foraging for free foods such as fungi, berries, and salad stuffs. Take great care what you eat when traveling since some plants that are highly poisonous may resemble familiar edible plants at home; ask local advice. There is a plant, for example, which provides succulent berries to foragers in Madagascar and looks almost identical to European deadly nightshade (*Atropa belladonna*). Consequently there are numerous hospital admissions and some deaths in Malagasy people who have consumed deadly nightshade berries in France.

Hospitable people from India and Pakistan offer *paan* to their honored guests. This is specially prepared from a range of ingredients kept in a beautiful box, or bought from a street vendor's stall. It is comprised of a fresh green betel leaf (*Piper betel*), into which is put a smear of lime, a fragment of areca palm nut (*Areca catechu*), sometimes a piece of tobacco, sometimes marijuana, and often spices. The contents are then folded and stuffed into the mouth and may be chewed or held in the cheek for an hour or so. If the mix contains tobacco, your saliva will become fiery and unswallowable which is why *paan*-chewers spit a lot, and the saliva becomes alarmingly, blood-red. Your host can modify the contents of your *paan* according to your tastes, and it is not impolite to request a less toxic concoction. There is some risk of filth-to-mouth or even water-borne infection from street-stall *paan* since the betel leaves are usually kept fresh by soaking in undesirable water and the vendor's hands are not always clean.

Eating a very sweet dish in Brazil, I asked what it was. My host said, "It's called Lady's Saliva and it's made from coconut milk, whole raw eggs, and sugar." Then in Japan I ate dried jellyfish that had been cut into strips; it looked like elastic bands, had the consistency of elastic bands, but with less flavor.

◆

*Dr. Charles Bangham, 44, medical research scientist, Imperial College School of Medicine, London, UK*

It is impossible to mention all possible chemical poisons that can contaminate food. However, since most naturally occurring food toxins are well recognized wherever they are consumed, local culinary habits have evolved to deal with them. Perhaps the most commonly eaten plant that is potentially toxic is the cassava; it is also called manioc. Tapioca is made from the cassava tuber. In its raw form it contains sufficient cyanide to kill, but local methods of preparation (boiling, soaking, washing in running water, and pounding) reduce the amount of cyanide to a nontoxic level. Do not prepare cassava yourself but get a local person to cook it for you. It is only a risky food during disasters or famine when there is insufficient time or fuel for traditional methods of preparation.

In Madagascar, people eat wood-encased, cricket-ball-sized fruits of trees that are closely related to *Strychnos nux-vomica*, the source of strychnine. Although the fruits are very tasty, eating lots will bring on a headache, a symptom perhaps of mild intoxication. Interestingly, overindulgence in the Sri Lankan "wood apple" (which looks superficially similar to *Strychnos*) also induces a headache; perhaps it also contains some tiny amount of toxin.

## *Tips*

➤ Many people who are traveling independently long term think that they need to take vitamin supplements. Vitamin deficiencies are most unlikely even on the dullest of diets unless you have very persistent, long-running diarrhea. Generally, those eating and absorbing sufficient calories also absorb sufficient vitamins and are unlikely to suffer deficiency syndromes. Seek a varied diet, though; it is good for the sake of both your mental and physical health.

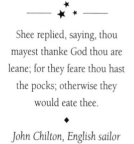

Shee replied, saying, thou mayest thanke God thou are leane; for they feare thou hast the pocks; otherwise they would eate thee.

◆

*John Chilton, English sailor in Mexico (1569)*

- If you are in doubt about the safety of a new or weird food, ask locals about it, and do not overindulge yourself at first.

- Most weird foods will be safe to eat—if unaesthetic—once they have been well cooked and are served hot.

- Beef or yak raised in less-than-sanitary conditions may carry tapeworm that will infest you unless the meat is thoroughly cooked.

- Avoid eating red or brightly colored fruits and berries unless you know them to be harmless.

- Never eat anything which looks like a tomato (unless you know it is one), even if it smells pleasant.

- Do not eat roots, fruits, or vegetables with a bitter, stinging, or otherwise disagreeable taste. Try them with the tip of your tongue if in doubt.

- Consuming uncooked wild watercress in regions where

The Chinese like to be absolutely sure that their food is fresh. They like to see their chickens killed in front of them and that any seafood was alive moments before consumption. The most revolting dish I've eaten—and I am unsure how it was prepared—was a fish served up still gasping but with its flesh cooked. Drunken prawns are similarly fresh. They are put into spirit alcohol where they swim until they die, and then eaten raw. I've been given "Bull's Stamina," which turned out to be penis, "three-snake soup" (quite tasty), and boiled sheep's ear (rather chewy). One of the most dangerous foods to eat in China is the steamed meat dumplings served by street vendors. These are not kept hot enough and are highly likely to make you ill; even the Chinese are wary of them.

◆

*Philip Andrews-Speed, 44, lecturer in international energy policy, Dundee University, Scotland*

freshwater is polluted carries a risk of liver fluke infestation.

➤ Seaweeds are all edible as long as you are not in a highly polluted area. The tastiest kinds are generally the pink, purple, reddish, or green types.

➤ Do not eat small wild birds in Papua New Guinea or Indonesian Irian Jaya.

➤ The liver of dogs, bears, and other carnivores is so loaded with vitamin A as to be toxic. Don't eat it.

➤ Cannibals in the Eastern Highlands of Papua New Guinea suffered slow neurological decline over months or years because they ate the brains of their victims. The disease, kuru, was due to a virus akin to the agents causing Creutzfeldt-Jakob or "mad cow" disease, and appeared after ten to twenty years incubation. Such "slow virus" infections come from eating brain, bone marrow, liver, or spleen of infected animals (or people).

---

A grateful farmer in the hills of East Nepal offered me a drink, but I wasn't thirsty so I declined. He was keen to press his hospitality and offered to mix yogurt with the amber fluid. I refused again and so he offered sugar too. It was only then that I realized that the drink was fresh cow's urine. It is taken locally for its healing properties.

◆

*Simon Howarth, 45, civil engineer, Cambridge, UK*

---

## Chapter 5

# SQUAT LOOS AND LONG-DROPS
## WHICH WAY TO THE LADIES/GENTS?

Written on a wall in one roundhouse
(the military slang for lavatory) was:
"This bloody roundhouse is no good at all
The seat is too high and the hole is too small!"

Underneath was added in a different hand:
"to which I must add the obvious retort.
Your arse is too large and your legs are too short!"

*— Found by "an eccentric potter from Ireland"*
*in a book by Alaistair Mars*

*P*erhaps one of *the* most awkward experiences of traveling is to enter a place that you understood was a toilet and then are unsure what to do or where or how to "go." You might even wonder whether you are in the lavatory at all. Exotic toilets come in many designs according to local needs, resources, and practices. Many look like a hole in the floor and the simplest is the long-drop— not a giraffe doing a poo but often slats over a simple dry pit. Such arrangements look primitive to those of us used to sitting

LOST: one Petzl headtorch in the long-drop, Horombo hut, Mount Kilimanjaro. Don't bother looking down there—that's what I was doing when it fell off.

♦

*Steve Foreman, 47, explorer,*
*Nottinghamshire, UK*

on thrones to ease ourselves, but simple squat latrines are practical, cheap, and hygienic in warmer climates that make conventional pedestal toilets difficult to keep clean and odor-free. The best squat loos are made of porcelain, have a water seal and have a cistern to flush away your offerings, but often there is only a bucket. In parts of Asia there are hybrid toilets halfway between a squat plate design and a pedestal. There is somewhere to squat or you can fold down a seat and sit to shit.

Flush toilets might seem to be an essential part of civilized living, and indeed they have existed for a very long time. Excavations in the 5,000-year-old city of Mohenjo-daro in Pakistan have revealed flush privies and a comprehensive system of town drainage. Flush toilets are popular in the West and so development agencies often build them in remote places. Some well-meaning organization built flush toilets at the hospital in Leh, Ladakh, at 11,000 feet in the western

The Tanzanian village had a toilet, a stone building with a boarded floor and a slit to squat over. Curious, I pointed a flashlight down the hole which revealed a seething mass of maggots some ten feet below. I should not have been surprised. The maggots were doing a good disposal job—there was very little smell.

◆

*Yvonne Robson, 41, veterinary surgeon, Simon's Town, South Africa*

"Are there toilets here?" I asked in my best Italian.

"*Si, signore,*" he replied pointing to a block of public lavatories. There was a door marked SIGNORE. "Signore means Sir, so that must be the Gents," I thought, so in I went. It was full of women! I beat a hasty retreat. Signore means Sir, but Signore also means Women! The word for Men is SIGNORI.

◆

*David White, 65, retired headmaster, Ayrshire, Scotland*

Himalayas. During the winter the maximum daytime temperature hovers around 14°F/-10°C so the flush toilets didn't flush and were not a success. A dry composting lavatory would have been more appropriate, and meanwhile traditional toilets continue to work extremely well. These are usually a hole in the floor of a house where soil from the fields is heaped into the corner. People crap into the hole, then toss down soil on top thus keeping the toilet almost odor-free. The excreta is naturally freeze-dried by the harsh climate and then in the spring it is dug out and used as fertilizer. My only problem with these is that they are often built into the highest point in the house, and sometimes there was a real feeling of vertigo on looking down several stories between my legs.

Locals using tropical squat loos usually use water to clean themselves, and there should be a tap or bucket for this and also to flush the toilet. Before you squat, check whether the tap functions or that there is some water in the bucket; pre-wetting the pan makes flushing easier.

Being tall, short-haired, with a fancy bicycle, I was obviously a man, whose insistence on using Ladies' lavatories in China was unacceptable. Women barred my way. "Go away. This is the Ladies!" they cried. "But I am a woman!" I insisted, and pushed past them. Crouching in the usual doorless cubicle, I was surrounded by gaping women. There were muffled exclamations. "Hey, get a look at this, sisters! It is a woman!" And how to tell which is the Ladies' in China? The Chinese character for "woman" looks very much like a person with her legs desperately crossed.

♦

*Catherine Hopper, 37, cycling Buddhist, Manchester, UK*

Some of the most disgusting loos I've used are squat toilets built for tourists in Nepal who, it seemed, were too idle to carry a little water to flush away their mess. In countries where water is scarce people are most inventive about other means of

33

cleaning their bottoms. In parts of Africa, scratchy corn (maize) husks are used for anal cleaning and subsequently tossed into the long-drop. This has pro-duced design dilemmas for development workers: latrine pits need to be bigger to accom-modate all the husks.

Squat toilets are usually key-hole-shaped and some have raised places to put your feet, but it is not always obvious which way round you should face. People are baffled about which way to face in a squat toi-let because there is no ideal. Generally if you are having a pee you need to face the hole and for more substantial movements you need your back to the hole. The footprint shapes in some squat toilets seem to be there to confuse the uninitiated. Before you decide what you are going to do, be warned: these toilets are designed for squatting. If you don't—or can't—squat (your knees may be seized after a Himalayan trek), whatever comes out of your tail end will splash on your shoes and lower garments. You also need to pull your pants and underwear down further than usual. This often deposits whatever is in your pockets into the toilet. Beware: recovering these treasures will not be an attractive maneuver.

Often toilets can be identified by being smelled from a dis-

In Eastern Europe many toilets are marked by ∇ for men and Δ for women; to remember which is which, put a circle for a head above each triangle, then think of women wearing skirts and broad-shouldered men.

♦

*Richard Lockhart, Šihulihi, Lithuania*

In the Baltic States, they go further and put the "heads" on the triangles for you so that foreigners will know where they stand, so to speak.

♦

*Simon Cave, 61, retired translator and inveterate traveler, Richmond, Surrey, UK*

tance, but it can be difficult deciding whether the lavatory you need is for men or women. In China this is often no problem since you can see the clientele inside, but in countries unused to foreigners the signs may be in another script or in code. Some pubs and restaurants can confuse visitors in trying to be amusing in the way they label the toilets. In Cornwall one pub indicates the door to the toilets with *YerTiz* (which translates as Here It Is). Then Neil Dixon found a seafood restaurant where they were labeled Buoys (boys) and Gulls (girls), and in Texas he was alarmed to see the Gents signed as Steers (castrated bulls) while the Ladies were insultingly called Heifers (young cows). In order to be able to identify the correct door in another establishment you needed to know which breed of dog was a *pointer* and which a *setter*. In Kerala the code is easier to break but you may emerge with delusions of grandeur: toilets there are labeled "kings" and "queens." Maybe the thing to do is just watch who enters which door.

Paid a visit to the loo at the airport in Ulan Bator; the signs were those silly international ones with a picture of a girl with a skirt and the man with the trousers. There I was washing my hands when an elderly man wearing the traditional *del*, comes into the loo, he looks around, very puzzled, looks at me wearing trousers, looks at himself wearing the long flowing skirted article, sighs, and retires into a cubicle to face his next hazard: a Western toilet.

♦

*Wendy Bentall, 55, editor of the* Scientific Exploration Society *newsletter, Chobham, Surrey, UK*

## Tips

➢ Before using any kind of basic lavatory, check whether there is water to flush it afterwards. You may need to go and fill the bucket yourself before your performance.

➤ Wet the pan of a squat toilet before use; this makes flushing easier and less messy.

➤ If there is a basket or bucket supplied for used toilet paper, please use it; it is the way to keep basic Third World plumbing functional.

➤ Asians often blame toilet blockages on use of toilet paper, but it is usually due to using inadequate volumes of water for flushing. Many travelers pour just enough water for the turd to slip down the hole, yet most lavatories need a good bucketful to make it flow smoothly as far as the sewer or septic tank.

➤ Public toilets may be scarce or squalid so make good use of facilities in cafés, hotels, bars, or restaurants when you get the chance.

In South America, the pipes that take away toilet effluent are not designed to cope with anything but excreta. In most public bathrooms there is a revolting basket full of used toilet paper. Put yours in there too rather than down the loo or you will block the pipes.

◆

*Peter Hutchison, 32, author, London, UK*

We'd been working as volunteer doctors and were taking in a few East African sights before heading home penniless. We intended smuggling our last few dollars across the border, and I'd slipped our last notes into my underpants in case we were searched. When I retired to the long-drop, I dropped my pants and the dollar bills fell into the pit. They were gone and I was in tears.

◆

*Dr. Sue Holmes, 41, general practitioner, Cambridge, UK*

➤ Always secure your pockets and your belt before entering a loo, however much of a hurry you might be in.

➤ Women will find full skirts are easier to "go" in than pants or dungarees, and they cover the essentials if the lavatory door is missing or inadequate.

➤ Hole-in-the-floor toilets are designed to be used in the squatting position. Squatting down low will reduce splashing, and you will emerge pristine if you can perfect the squat! Squatting is very good for the hip joints and is the proper physiological position for moving the bowels. Practice at home before you depart. Work at your balance and flexibility, and strengthen your thigh muscles.

➤ Stand clear when pulling the flush to empty the cistern. The plumbing may wet more than the pan.

I had a dose of the runs and had to use a typically disgusting, fly-infested squat loo in a Peruvian café. As I positioned myself over the hole and dropped my drawers, there was a dull thud. My treasured Swiss army knife and its leather pouch (blessed by the Bishop of Guadalajara) had slipped from my belt. I rolled up my sleeve, plunged my arm up to the elbow into the most appalling mess and with an almighty squelch retrieved my knife. That day there was no running water.

♦

*Hallam Murray, 49, who cycled 17,000 miles from California to Tierra del Fuego, London, UK*

➤ Some basic long-drop toilets have a cover to close the hole. Keeping this in place reduces the numbers of mosquitoes and flies inside; be sure to replace the cover after use. And then wash your hands.

- ➤ When squatting to defecate, face the slim end of the keyhole shape.

- ➤ In parts of Southeast Asia, people believe they are invisible when bathing or shitting and so are not embarrassed by spectators; consequently, toilets are not always as private as you might like; ancient Romans saw going to the public latrine as a social event and would sit around chatting while moving their bowels.

- ➤ When new to a country, ask fellow travelers how the men's toilets are distinguished from the women's; you will hear some interesting tales.

Driving to Brittany, I used a hole-in-the-ground toilet with footpads; as soon as I put my feet on the pads, it flushed, soaking my new sandals. In another English-style toilet, as soon as you got near the seat it flushed and continued flushing: very off-putting when you are having a wee. Then I got soaked again entering an outdoor swimming pool. I was carrying a towel and t-shirt. As soon as I put my foot in the footbath to enter, a hoop of shower jets soaked me from above. Aggh! French plumbing!

◆

*Josephine Thomas, 64, retired secretary and tennis player, Surrey, UK*

---

Rules for ladies using Greek "squatties":
Door (if provided) should be firmly locked.
Shorts or skirt should be removed and clutched in teeth.
Panties should be removed and tucked into bra.
Body parts should be matched to the apertures in the porcelain.
The performance may now commence.
On completion, replace clothes, flush and run like hell.

◆

*Jean McRonald, 60, doctor's receptionist, Monifieth, Dundee, Scotland*

*Chapter 6*

# WATER, WATER
## DEHYDRATION, REHYDRATION

Some folks die of whisky, and some folks die of beer,
And some folks di-a-betes, and some of di-a-rrhea…

*— Anonymous*

---

*E*ven the wisest and most meticulously careful traveler can be struck by diarrhea, so it pays to know about its treatment. Diarrhea is an outpouring from the bowel and in its severest form can make you "go" more than a dozen times a day. It so confuses the intestine that all-essential fluids pour out of your backside or get pooled in places that are of no immediate use to your body, skulking unavailable somewhere within your abdomen. The key challenge when you begin a bout of diarrhea, then, is to replace the lost or sequestered fluid. Yet this is a time when you may not feel like drinking or eating anything. You may feel nauseated, you may even be

"He looks awful: feeling dizzy, can hardly get out of bed, terrible diarrhea, splitting headache. He thinks he's dying. Could it be cholera?"

◆

*Phone call from a diarrhea-sufferer's friend, Hyderabad, Pakistan*

vomiting, and your abdomen may be bloated by pooled fluid and excess gas. So what do you do? You must drink.

During diarrhea, the stomach and intestines do not absorb fluids very efficiently: your body's normal physiological mecha-

39

nisms need some assistance. Absorption is most efficient—even when you are vomiting—if fluids are taken as a mixture of water, salt, and a carbohydrate (such as sugar, glucose, or even starch). The body will be hungry for that sugar and salt, and in pulling that across the stomach wall, water will also be dragged into your bloodstream—to where it is needed. The easiest way of taking such a sugar and salt solution is to open a packet of Oral Rehydration Salts (ORS), dissolve it in clean water, and then drink a couple of large glasses after each time you open your bowels. You can drink more if you are thirsty. Many wise travelers pack a few ORS packets when they are heading for less-hygienic environments (see page 131 for the contents of my minimal medical kit). ORS packets are also widely available in little medicine shops in the developing world. Sometimes the language on the packet may not be one you can read but someone should be able to help—in Thailand the script is unintelligible but the solution is still called *oh-are-ess*. These packets are usually added to one glass or one liter of water (and it is

It must have been the food at the wedding in Bandarej, Rajasthan. My stomach started to give warning signals, I christened a rooftop, then took a rickshaw back to the hotel, stopping three times en route to empty my stomach. The doctor declared me well-and-truly dehydrated, started an intravenous drip, gave me "a little prick" in the bottom and organized a nurse who force-fed me bananas and oral rehydration solution while our local friends prayed for us. I wouldn't choose any other place to be ill in.

◆

*Margaret Rivera, 59¾,*
*recycled teenager, Lincoln, UK*

important to be sure which!) but in Thailand the packet was designed for dissolution in 750 ml, which is about three good-sized glasses of water. Fortunately the pharmacist was helpful

and anyway the only compre-
hensible script on the packet
was "750." It is important to get
the volume right; improperly
made up solution can do more
harm than good. If in doubt,
overdilute.

If ORS packets are not available, then you can make your
own sugar and salt solution. You
can mix:

If diarrhea or heat overcome
you while in India, one way to
revive yourself is by taking the
locally available Vijay
Electrolyte (a mix of salt and
dextrose) with water.

♦

*James O'Reilly and
Larry Habegger,*
Travelers' Tales India

- Two heaped (generous) teaspoons of glucose or sugar or
  honey and a three-finger pinch (less than a quarter teaspoon) of salt in a glass of boiled and cooled water.

-or-

- Eight level teaspoons (or four heaped teaspoons) of glucose
  or sugar or honey plus a level teaspoon of salt in a liter.

- In addition to sugar and salt you can also add a squeeze of
  orange, lemon, or lime juice which makes the drink taste
  better and also adds potassium, which is lost from the body
  during diarrhea and vomiting.

- The solution should taste no more salty than tears.

Normally you obtain a lot of fluid from your food, about
three liters a day. If you are feeling too ill to eat, then you need
to drink three liters *plus* whatever is disappearing down the
toilet plus (and this is especially important if you are in a hot
climate or have a fever) water losses from sweat. It is all too
easy to become dehydrated and this—above all—is what

makes you feel awful when your stomach is upset. Dizziness and headache can both be symptoms of dehydration, so see whether drinking makes you feel better.

When I have the shits, I like to take a variety of fluids, and a good light novel. I often start on a stomach-settling cola (with a pinch of salt added), but I rapidly tire of sweet drinks. My favorite is hot lemon (to which I add a little salt and some sugar), but I also like drinks made from bouillon cubes (with a little sugar added), and very weak black teas and infusions. I am always on the lookout for concoctions of clear fluids that are not sweet for these times of serious drinking.

"Simple" travelers' diarrhea can cause considerable problems if you have any ongoing medical condition or are taking any regular medication. Diabetics particularly may become quite unwell with diarrhea as the demands of the illness increase insulin requirements. And, it is all right for diabetics to drink ORS and homemade oral rehydration solutions, despite the fact they contain glucose or sucrose.

Children and older travelers can become very unwell surprisingly quickly, because they may be less capable of maintaining electrolyte balance. Take no risks if you are traveling with any of these special groups: get properly briefed by your physician before departure, ideally take a travel health book too, and seek medical help early in case of problems.

Lack of understanding of the importance of drinking is the most common health "mistake" I encounter in travelers, and an example follows about a man I met in Nepal. The dry-lipped American was coming down from the Thorong La on Annapurna; he was so unwell and exhausted they'd put him on a horse. He looked haggard; he had diarrhea. I offered help. "You are quite dehydrated and that makes you feel bad. You need to drink liters to replace the losses from diarrhea and from breathing hard at altitude."

"I drank a quart this morning and also a glass of that oral rehydration stuff so I'm not dehydrated." But he was dehydrated. He ordered a Coke and I suggested he add a pinch of salt to it to improve absorption. "Look—I got all the salts I need from that packet...."

He misunderstood that together salt and sugar (whether in the form of ORS or salt added to cola) are a vehicle for fluid absorption, not a one-off treatment. Proper continuing rehydration would have made him feel better surprisingly quickly but he was too miserable, too unwell to want to listen. Yet he was feeling unnecessarily awful.

# *Tips*

➤ When you have diarrhea it is important to drink lots (liters) to replace lost fluids.

➤ Any *clear* fluid is good for rehydrating but mixtures of sweet and salt are best.

➤ Avoid milk when you have diarrhea; it can lead to a temporary allergy to milk sugar (lactose).

➤ Rehydrate with a glass of boiled and cooled water containing two heaped teaspoons of glucose or sugar or honey and a three-finger pinch (less than a quarter teaspoon) of salt and a squirt

When trekking in the Himalayas, always keep a couple of plastic bags by the side of your bed. If food poisoning sets in there is just not enough time to fight your way out of a well-done-up sleeping bag and run to the toilet.

◆

*Lauren Proctor, 25, adventurer, Sedbergh, Lancashire*

of lemon, lime, or orange juice. Brown sugar, molasses, or in India *gur* can be used instead of sugar—such "impure" forms of sugar are actually better than refined sugar since they are rich in potassium which is lost (and needs to be replaced) during diarrhea and vomiting.

➤ Add a pinch of salt to your Coke or Fanta or cordial: it sounds revolting but drinking it will make you feel a whole lot better. Lemon squash drink or hot lemon with sugar and salt added is also a good rehydration solution.

➤ Other good rehydration solutions are rice-water, clear soups, young coconut, drinks made from Marmite, Vegemite, Bovril or bouillon cubes, herbal infusions, Malagasy *ranovola*, South American chamomile tea (*manzanilla*), hot lemon and lemon tea, herbal teas, weak black tea, and very weak black coffee may also be taken. Beware of hot drinks, though: they will make you want to "go."

➤ Oral rehydration salts, ORS, are available in most countries: *Electrolade, Dioralyte, Rehidrat*, etc. in the UK, *Oralit* in Indonesia, and *Jeevan Jal* (literally water of life) in Nepal. ORS is best for children, the frail, those with long-standing medical problems, and also anyone with profuse (twelve times a day) diarrhea.

➤ When you have diarrhea, aim to drink two large glasses of clear fluid after each time you have opened your bowels and drink more if you feel thirsty. Most people will need to drink and drink.

➤ Some people find alternative treatments work well for them including homeopathy, traditional Chinese medicine, etc., but these should be taken in combination with plenty to drink. Some so-called alternative practitioners in Asia are quacks, and in Sri Lanka I have seen practitioners who called themselves Ayurvedic handing out Valium and antibiotics.

➤ Dizziness, especially on getting out of bed or getting up from a chair, is a symptom of low blood pressure. When this is caused by dehydration, the treatment is to drink *several liters* of clear fluids.

➤ Headache is a symptom with innumerable causes, but if you have diarrhea it may indicate dehydration; try drinking two liters of ORS or other clear fluids to see whether that helps.

➤ Bananas help slow diarrhea, are easily digested, and also contain lots of potassium.

—— ✶ —— 

Before we'd started to taxi, I'd already filled six sick bags. I shouldn't have eaten the chicken salad. I only just made it to the toilet and escaped only twenty minutes later. By the time I next needed to use the lavatory, a queue had formed. Desperately I screamed "Emergency! Diarrhea!" and pushed through. Safe now, I nodded off to be awoken by a stewardess announcing, "The front toilet is temporarily out of action. Passengers should use toilets at the rear."

◆

*Jo Bourne, Olney, 31, frustrated teacher, Buckinghamshire, UK*

➤ Fluid requirements are increased to beyond three liters a day by: diarrhea, vomiting, sweating, fever, strenuous exercise, hot climate, being at high altitude, lactation, and some medications.

➤ If feeling unwell when on the bus, train, or plane, put a few plastic shopping bags in your pocket, just in case there is no *sac vomitoire* (as they are so delicately labeled on Air Madagascar flights). Sometimes the cabin crew cannot produce them fast enough.

- ➤ Alcoholic drinks should never be used to rehydrate after exercise or during diarrhea. Even beer stimulates the loss of more fluid than is replaced because of excessive urination.

- ➤ Well or not, always avoid drinking spirits before sundown. Alcohol in hot climates leads to dehydration and sometimes even severe sunburn.

For the Flux—Take the chokes off a pike's head so that the teeth stick in and burn them on a tiles stone and make powder thereof and drink it with stale ale or eat it in your pottage.

◆

*Unknown English author, perhaps Dame Juliana Berners, circa 1480*

A gentleman always carries a box of matches. The sulfur in a burning match seems to be the most potent remedy for bathroom smells: strike a couple and burn them down as far as you can, and the worst of the offense will be dissipated. Do not, whatever you do, hunt in the bathroom cabinet for unused scent and spray it around; the combination of perfume and pong is an effective emetic.

◆

*Serena, in* The Independent Newspaper, *UK*

## Chapter 7

# CAUGHT SHORT?
## MANAGING ON LONG BUS RIDES

*The boys retreated to a nearby fence. I crouched behind the largest boulder I could find. My audience perched on top of the fence to get as good a view as possible. When I pulled up my shorts they were grinning at me. They hung back. I knew, with a vague sense of humiliation, that they would examine the green mess I'd left behind, then make full report to all their cousins and friends.*

—*Tim Ward,* Travelers' Tales Nepal

---

*I*t was 1976. I'd survived my first Himalayan trek and had just returned to the civilization of Kathmandu. I hadn't eaten much for ten days. The diarrhea had finally settled down, but rice and lentil slop had been unenticing and my appetite had gone. When we went out for breakfast in Thamel though, the hot *rosti* made me drool; the portion was huge, dripping with fat and topped with melted cheese. I hadn't taken many mouthfuls before I realized I'd made a big mistake; this was not good food for a convalescing bowel. First there was a brisk gastro-colic reflex, then the nausea returned, and cramps kept me awake all night.

Rehydration—drinking liters of clear fluids—is the most important part of treating travelers' diarrhea, or dysentery or even cholera, but there are some other tips which will help control your symptoms so that you do not get caught short on the bus. The outpouring of gut contents which is diarrhea happens when the intestine is in a hurry to push out toxic mush;

often the gut is in such a hurry that it goes into spasm and causes abdominal pains. These come and go (a constant pain is more likely due to another cause) and are often relieved by opening the bowels or passing wind. These kinds of cramps are common in diarrheal disease, but eating small quantities of bland foods can reduce them. Pure carbohydrates are best (boiled potatoes, rice, couscous, or plain crackers), and these also assist absorption of fluids if you drink plenty of water with them. Greasy or spicy foods will make cramps worse and so will very heavy meals. If you don't feel like eating, your body is probably giving you good advice: stick to clear fluids and a few dry crackers.

The physiological phenomenon called the gastro-colic reflex is something that travelers should understand. When any hot or very cold food or drink is swallowed, there is a reflex tendency for the bowels to open. Under normal circumstances this happens perhaps after breakfast when you need your daily evacuation. When you have diarrhea, however, this reflex becomes friskier and more difficult to control so that a mouthful of ice-cold cola or a spoonful of hot rice pudding will make you want to dash to the loo. If the diarrhea is bad, the trip will have been worthwhile but because all is not well, the reflex

Having succumbed first to altitude sickness and then to the dreaded diarrhea, I was resting up in a Kathmandu guest house. I was lying on my bunk one afternoon, reading, when an English trekker who had also been unwell comes bounding into the room gleefully.

"How's this for self-confidence?" he says, and lets fly with a terrifying English fart.

"No follow-through! No follow-through!" he chortles, leaping around the room.

◆

*Rob Hosking, 35, journalist and singer of bad country songs, New Zealand*

may produce little more than a damp fart. And the big problem is—especially if you are traveling by bus or a light aircraft without a toilet—when this reflex strikes you may not be able to tell whether you'll have to go or whether you'll be able to hang on. If your intestines are ailing, then, avoid very hot drinks or foods or very cold or iced drinks. Aim to take any drinks at room temperature and allow food or hot drinks to cool before consumption.

On buses and coaches in the tropics you can usually persuade the driver to pull over if you need to stop, although he is not going to be very impressed if you ask him to stop every fifteen minutes. Yet even with an obliging driver, finding a place to "go" can be a problem. You can be sure that most suitable places beside the road on a busy bus route will be polluted and unpleasant and often there is little cover. I try to travel in a long loose skirt when I'm doing long bus trips in Asia or Africa so that if there is no cover at all I can just squat at the side of the road, spread my skirts, and evacuate unobserved.

A good medicine for the colic—
Take the hulls of green beans
and distil them and make water
thereof and use that fasting
with a little stale ale until
you are eased thereof.

♦

*Unknown English author,*
*possibly Dame Juliana Berners,*
*circa 1480*

Fluids and a bland diet will be all the treatment that is needed for most attacks of the shits, but if you have diarrhea that has gone on for more than three days, it would be wise to organize a stool test if you can. Medical laboratories in the tropics may have few resources but usually they are experts at stool examination. Make sure the sample is fresh—that means still warm. Almost any laboratory can manage to look at the sample under a microscope. If they see mucus or red blood cells (written RBC; a following "+" indicates RBC have been seen; "++" quite a few are present; or "+++" means that the technician has seen lots), this indicates dysentery which requires antibiotic treatment (see pages 55 and 56). The kind of antibiotic depends upon the nature of the symptoms and not the laboratory result. Presence of worms eggs may be another finding, but these do not do any harm (and do not usually cause diarrhea) so you can wait for treatment until it is convenient and you trust the doctors. More sophisticated laboratories can identify bacteria and work out which antibiotic will kill that bacteria most effectively. This process takes some days, and often you will be better by the time you get the result...or you will be in the next town. A simple look under the microscope is all you need unless you are very unwell with a high fever and/or some serious problem like typhoid is suspected.

Many travelers carry antidiarrheal medicines with them such as loperamide (Imodium or Arret), Lomotil (a morphinelike drug), or codeine phosphate. These medicines do not treat the underlying cause of the diarrhea but reduce the frequency of needing to stop the bus. Personally though, I feel worse taking these drugs because those noxious microbes are kept inside for longer. Furthermore, these "blocking" drugs are dangerous if you have dysentery, if you have certain ongoing

On an eighteen-seater Royal Nepal Twin Otter flight nonstop to Surkhet, I noticed a fellow passenger go into the cockpit to have an earnest conversation with the pilot. Soon we landed on an unfamiliar grass airstrip; the poor Japanese passenger made a dash for some bushes close to the runway, then reboarded the plane looking much happier.

♦

*Simon Howarth, 45, irrigation engineer, then-resident in Rajapur Island, West Nepal*

medical problems, or if they are given to a child. I don't like them. Generally, by taking a minimal bland diet and lots of fluids, trips to the toilet diminish, and most of the symptoms will be gone in thirty-six hours. If my diarrhea were bad, I'd delay the bus ride for twenty-four hours until the symptoms were more manageable.

Be careful about what you take from local pharmacies. Some banned drugs like the quinolone Enterovioform are still available in developing countries. Drugs like chloramphenicol (sold as Chloromycetin, Catilan, or Enteromycetin) and the sulfa antibiotics (e.g., Streptomagma) work well but they have too many serious side

The bus trip through central Ethiopia had been hard going. So had the evening meal of tough goat meat. At 2 A.M. I awoke with cramps in my stomach. The vicious dog that was tied to a high stake between me and the rough toilet shed snarled savagely. Only by making him chase in circles around the pole could I shorten his rope enough to safely edge past and eventually reach the old tin bog-house. If the dog's snarling hadn't woken the dead, then my loud explosive outpouring certainly would have.

◆

*Bob Maysmor, 50, museum professional, Wellington, New Zealand*

effects to be worth the risk in treating simple diarrhea. Do not take any of these unless there are specific indications.

## *Tips*

➤ The most important part of treating diarrhea is to drink large amounts of clear fluids.

➤ Drink two large glasses of ORS or other clear fluid after each bowel movement.

- Mixtures of sugar and salt in water are better absorbed than plain water so try adding a pinch of salt to your cola.

- Avoiding very hot food or drinks and very cold food or iced drinks will make a delicate bowel less troublesome so that you should be able to manage that bus, boat, or light aircraft journey without resorting to medicines.

- If you have diarrhea and don't feel like eating, don't eat for a day but drink lots.

- Bland, high-carbohydrate diets are easy to digest and are good convalescent food; these are crackers, bread, boiled rice, couscous, or potatoes.

- Avoid taking drugs unless a reputable practitioner has prescribed them.

- Never take "blockers" like Lomotil or Imodium if passing blood with the stools and never give these paralytic drugs to children.

The rickety bus had jolted for hours along the mountain roads of Luzon, Philippines. When the driver drew up beside a roadside restaurant, my daughter and I joined the women, all holding toilet rolls, in a mad dash to a concrete hut. We were confronted with twelve holes in an L-shaped pattern. Absolutely no privacy, and barely room to squat without bumping elbows or bottoms!

◆

*Jane Vincent-Havelka, over 60, travel writer, London, Ontario, Canada*

In China, I met a fellow backpacker who'd been unable to evacuate his colon for eleven days. "Better take these then," I said, and helpfully gave him two tablets. Later I noticed I'd given him Imodium.

◆

*Jeremy Garner, 28, constipated copywriter, London, UK*

- Wait at least twelve hours before taking any "cure"—except (of course) oral rehydration.

- Seek medical advice if you have severe abdominal pain, can't drink, or feel very unwell.

- Abdominal pains associated with diarrhea are less worrying if evacuating or passing gas relieves the pain.

- Some people are left with "irritable bowel syndrome" after a tropical trip and its associated gastrointestinal unease. This diagnosis can only reliably be made after excluding *Giardia* infection; this is detected or excluded by examination of three separate fresh stool samples.

- Long-lasting mild diarrhea can be a symptom of stress, in which case the holistic, alternative therapies can be very helpful.

I don't know if this was true but a diplomat told me this story in 1984. Chap on his way to catch a train in Delhi suffering from diarrhea soiled himself. He dashed into a shop, gesticulated to the assistant that he needed new pants, had them wrapped and rushed to catch the train. He cleaned himself up in the toilet, tossed the soiled pants out of the window, and opened the parcel to find he'd bought a shirt.

◆

*Neal Robbins, 45, journalist, Cambridge, UK*

Hot back from a tropical trip with some unwanted hitchhikers, I visited the toilet. Diarrhea. Not confident in maintaining continence throughout the session in court, I stuffed a load of lavatory paper into my underwear, just in case. I was called to the witness box to give my evidence and noticed the court reporters stifling laughter behind their notepads. No wonder, a length of pink loo paper emerged from my trouser leg, and trailed down the steps and across the courtroom.

◆

*Steve Foreman, 47, former detective, Walesby, Nottinghamshire, UK*

# Chapter 8

# TROUBLESOME KINDS OF GASTROENTERITIS

## DYSENTERY AND MORE SERIOUS KINDS OF DIARRHEA

The English—ah the English. They are renowned for the frailty of
their digestive systems and their preoccupation with drains and
plumbing. They have a talent for diarrhoea…if an Englishman
hasn't got it, he's looking for somewhere to have it.

—*Peter Mayle, A Year in Provence*

———

*T*ravelers' diarrhea is the most common gastrointestinal
ailment of travelers, but if you allow other peoples'
feces into your mouth, you risk other filth-to-mouth
infections. Yuck, you say—never. But it is hard to avoid unhy-
gienically prepared food, and when you do eat it, there are
more diseases on the menu at the same restaurant. These may
not cause diarrhea, but they will make you ill, and many need
proper antibiotic treatment. The good news is that the prevention strategies for almost all of these fecal-oral diseases are similar. The vast majority reach you through contaminated foods,
so all should be avoidable by following the advice in Chapter 1.
Initially, treatments too are similar. Most bouts of diarrhea will
stop within seventy-two hours, and fluid replacement (see
Chapter 6) is the only treatment you will require. However,
some microbes can cause quite a deal of discomfort and illness,
and the following notes are to help you decide whether you
need more treatment than oral rehydration. There follows,

then, some details of the more common infections, or those that fascinate travelers.

Explosive diarrhea that comes on suddenly, often with a fever and, sometimes, visible blood in the stool, suggests bacterial or **bacilliary dysentery**, usually due to *Shigella*. It definitely will ruin your day and is best treated with oral rehydration therapy and antibiotics. If you can, go to a doctor but if none is available, consider taking a three-day course of one of the following antibiotics: ciprofloxacin, norfloxacin, or nalidixic acid. These are unsuitable for people with epilepsy, liver or kidney disease, and in pregnancy; take medical advice before treating children. Dramatic watery diarrhea should also respond to this kind of treatment. Whether or not you take antibiotics, rehydration is still a very important part of therapy. These antibiotics will also work well for many of the microbes causing significant (that is, going more than six times a day) diarrhea in travelers although since much of the diarrhea we acquire at home is viral, antibiotics are no help and could even make the situation worse. Don't use these treatment guidelines for symptoms you experience at home.

Bloody diarrhea without fever is often **amebic dysentery**.

02.00 hours. Awoken by a twinge from my rear gunner. Chocks away! Airborne, hovering over target…fire! Payload deployed.

03.00 hours. Log alert! Sure this time my sheets would meet their Agincourt as bomb doors open prematurely. Hurling battle-fatigued cheeks onto target with thunderous roars. Mission completed…but such is the unpredictability of war (and Fijian curries), I stayed awake on sentry duty until morning. As dawn broke, lavatorial friendly fire was confirmed: my sheets were a right old Officers' Mess.

◆

*Matt Collier, 26,
advertising consultant,
Blackheath, London, UK*

This requires treatment with oral rehydration therapy and tinidazole (for five days) or, if this is not available, metronidazole (Flagyl) tablets. Amebic dysentery tends to come on insidiously, in great contrast to the spectacular onset of bacterial diarrheas.

*Giardia* is a beautiful heart-shaped parasite that causes **giardiasis.** It swims the breaststroke around the intestinal contents. As a side effect of its activity it produces large quantities of sulfurous gas. This distends the abdomen, causes cramps, and exits as eggy belches and foul-smelling farts. This little beastie will cause you little harm, but no one will want to share a tent with you when you have giardiasis. You may take tinidazole or, if this is not available, a short course of metronidazole (Flagyl) to get rid of it.

**Cyclospora** causes diarrhea that is seldom severe, but untreated, comes and goes over as much as twelve weeks. It causes noticeable weight loss: of eleven to twenty-two pounds. Treatment is with co-trimoxazole (Septran, Bactrim, etc.), but this antibiotic is unsuitable for those who are allergic to sulfa drugs. If this does not help, you should certainly head for a reputable medical center and consult a doctor. It is a "new" illness, originally confused with blue-green algae but now recognized as another parasite that forms spores and so it is not eradicated from drinking water by iodine or other chemicals.

*En famille* in Bali, my seventeen-year-old son got the trots and (despite all the traveling we'd done) claimed he'd never felt so ill before. I ignored his complaints and he got better — slowly. Six weeks later he was ill again, and again a month or so after that. It turned out to be his appendix. Montezuma's revenge can be more than simple diarrhea.

♦

*Ro Dawson, 51, publisher,*
*Footprint Handbooks,*
*Bath, England*

**Typhoid** is a nasty infection that wise travelers should know a little about. It is not particularly common, with travelers from the United States acquiring the infection at the estimated rate of only about 6 cases per million journeys. Trips to tropical Latin America and the Indian subcontinent carry a higher risk: about 174 cases per million journeys arise from returnees from Peru for example, and these figures do not count the similar paratyphoid A, B, and C infections. The symptoms of typhoid may begin with a temporary slight diarrhea and then after seven to fourteen days the fever begins; there then may be constipation. Often the fever increases steadily; there is usually a headache and feeling of being unwell. After a further week, the fever has become high, making the sufferer very unwell, and by the third week there is a danger of intestinal perforation. It is a disease requiring competent medical attention and proper antibiotic treatment. **Paratyphoid** is a similar but usually milder illness where diarrhea is a commoner symptom. Long-lasting gastrointestinal symptoms, especially with increasing fevers, should send you scampering for a doctor in a large town. **Typhus** also causes fever, but it is acquired from tick or louse bites, not the filth-to-mouth route.

Rumblings within made me ask my Sumatran hosts about the toilet, and they directed me outside. There I found a stinking pond with a narrow plank stretched across. Precariously fitted halfway along was a rickety old bamboo frame surrounded with cloth. I shuffled along the plank, ducked inside, dropped my shorts, grasped the flimsy bamboo, leaned back, and prayed.

♦

*Vincent Ward, 39, a true believer, Chiba-ken, Japan*

**Hepatitis** means inflammation of the liver from any cause. This often leads to jaundice, which means yellowing of the skin and the whites of the eyes. Two filth-to-mouth viral infections cause infective hepatitis; they are also known as hepatitis A and E. About a month after eating a contaminated meal, the first symptom is likely to be loss of appetite. There will be some mild fever, aches and pains, and then about a week later, as this all starts to settle, the yellowing becomes noticeable, the urine becomes dark in color and the feces pale. The jaundice should settle over several weeks. Complications or severe illness is rare, although it is common for sufferers to feel fatigued for weeks after the illness has subsided. There is a chance of severe illness in pregnant women, so pregnancy is not the time to visit regions of high filth-to-mouth disease transmission. This is a viral infection—antibiotics are of no help although Ayurvedic cures in India and Nepal, and Amchi remedies in Ladakh and Tibet, seem to improve symptoms.

Polio or **poliomyelitis** is a gastrointestinal infection that can leave sufferers with a paralyzed limb. Fortunately, though, this disease is on the decline and there is an effective vaccine.

**Cysticercosis** is the term for infestation with pork tapeworm cysts. If someone is unfortunate enough to eat pork tapeworm eggs through eating food contaminated with the feces of someone harboring a pork tapeworm, worm cysts can be laid down in the victim's muscles, under the skin, and even in the eye and brain. I have heard of this being a problem in people eating salads irrigated with raw sewage in South America: this is another reason for sticking to the "peel it, boil it, cook it, or forget it" motto.

**Cholera** is a disease that scares travelers, but well-nourished, healthy adults rarely get into trouble even if they do swallow some of these bacteria. It seems to cause disease only in the debilitated or if it infects people along with other microbes. And the same measures protect you from contracting it anyway. Don't worry about it.

There are other causes of diarrhea in travelers. Most notorious, perhaps, is **tropical sprue** which—untreated—can cause a persistent diarrhea that goes on for months and months. Don't let it. Seek medical help before you get run down and debilitated. It often gets better miraculously on getting home.

Finally, keep in mind that not all diarrhea in travelers is travelers' diarrhea: there are tropical causes like malaria and there are nontropical, noncommunicable causes that just happen to start while you are traveling. Sometimes it takes an expert to sort out a diagnosis so if you have continuing symptoms, seek a medical opinion. Don't take more than one course of prescription medicines without seeking a doctor's advice, and preferably at least one stool test.

## Tips

> Most so-called "simple" travelers' diarrhea will settle within thirty-six hours.

> You will feel much better by keeping well hydrated: drink lots of ORS or other clear fluids.

> If symptoms are severe or continue beyond seventy-two hours, seek medical advice if possible. Otherwise, if no doctor is available,

If you get the runs at Krakow railway station, you could be in trouble. Your two-sheet ration of loo paper, obtained from the attendant, costs 3,000 zloty (about 20 cents). Counting out that lot in 5- or 10-zloty notes takes time. In an emergency, make a run for it and use the zloty instead.

♦

*Angela Rowe, 49, musician/IT worker, Swansea Valley, Wales*

consider antibiotic treatment; antibiotics (with fluid replacement) are effective in treating the root cause of most travelers' diarrhea acquired in developing countries and these are generally safer medicines to take than "blockers" such as Imodium or Lomotil. They also avoid the uncomfortable side effect of rebound constipation after the diarrhea subsides.

➢ Fever, severe diarrhea of sudden onset with frequent explosive bowel movements (twelve times a day or more), blood in the stool, and feeling very unwell are all symptoms implying you have something that is more than "simple" travelers' diarrhea. They suggest that you have a form of diarrhea or dysentery that might persist and probably needs treatment with antibiotics.

➢ I have heard it said that you can catch typhoid from filthy bank notes; that will depend upon the purposes to which they have been put and also whether they go near your mouth. Travelers, don't forget to wash your hands with soap and plenty of water before eating.

➢ It is dangerous to treat dysentery (bloody diarrhea or severe diarrhea with fever) with "blocking" paralytic medicines such as Imodium or Lomotil. They can cause intestinal perforation.

➢ Not all diarrhea in travelers is travelers' diarrhea.

> —— ★ ★ ——
>
> 1976. Arrive in Baler, on remote NE Philippines coast, after grueling drive over the mountains and am astonished to find every hotel and restaurant full, and U.S. helicopter gunships roaring overhead. They are shooting *Apocalypse Now*. Forced to eat in a dubious dive where food has been exposed, gently warming, for hours. Get my apocalypse now—explosive dysentery—but live to enjoy the film.
>
> ◆
>
> *Rowena Quantrill, 57, writer and film-goer, Bradford-on-Avon, England*

➢ If you have recently returned home from the developing world, be aware that you could still be carrying microbes that will harm others if you allow them to reach another's mouth. This is especially likely if your bowels are still a little unsettled. In these circumstances, dispose of your excreta in a toilet or bury it even more meticulously when outdoors.

➢ Abdominal pain is common when traveling, and mostly it is mild and transient. Pain relieved by BMs or passing wind is usully benign. Appendicitis tends to start as central abdominal pain that progresses and settles in the right lower corner of the abdomen. Pains in the left lower corner of the abdomen are common in constipation and also when there is profuse diarrhea—this latter pain comes from a tired, cramped colon.

Many years ago I took a bus trip through Greece with some college classmates. Toward the end of the journey, I felt that I might be having an attack of appendicitis. I had severe abdominal pain, so severe I confided in a wise, old priest who was acting as a guide. He suggested a suppository.

"What for?" I asked. "I'm not constipated." But as the words tumbled out of my mouth a ray of hope presented itself. What if I was only constipated, and not dying of an unknown illness?

As soon as we got to Athens, I hastened to the pharmacy. Returning to my room, I gazed with loathing at the enormous object that I was supposed to insert into my backside. Reluctantly, yet with haste, as the abdominal pains surged, I bent to my task. Soon I was squatting over a hole in the marble floor of the bathroom, giving birth to an enormous pile of excrement that, like a mad termite colony or a volcano, could hardly be contained by the space in which it grew. Gazing with wonder at this ziggurat of colonic filth, I rose a new man, knowing with renewed clarity the meaning of resurrection.

◆

*Sean O'Reilly, 47, writer and editor, Peoria, Arizona*

Chapter 9

# IMMUNIZATION AGAINST DIARRHEA AND TRAVELERS' ILLS

## PRECAUTIONS NOW AND IN THE FUTURE

My bowels shall sound like an harp.

—*Isaiah, 16:11*

———

*T*his little book dwells upon those filth-to-mouth diseases that travelers risk, yet we can look forward to a time when the risks will be much less because immunization will be possible against many of these troublesome microbes. The first time people were immunized against a fecal-oral travelers' infection was in 1896 during the Boer War, when typhoid vaccine was given to protect British soldiers. It gave only partial protection in exchange for a very sore arm, fever, and often a headache, but it saved lives. That original "whole cell vaccine" was superseded only in the early 1990s by purer antigens comprising a genetically engineered element of bacterial cell wall. These cause fewer side effects, and there is also a choice of products so that now if you are one of the unfortunate 7 percent to get a sore arm after one typhoid vaccine, you can try the other. Or you can even take capsules—as long as you are prepared to pay six times as much in order to avoid the needle.

Many travelers are still immunized against typhoid,

although not all need it. The typhoid risk is highest in those visiting tropical Latin America or the Indian subcontinent. Some physicians would say that travelers to other regions do not need typhoid immunization, but this decision is also dependent upon how "rough" you are traveling. In the past the vaccine was a combined typhoid and paratyphoid A and B antigen (TAB); there is no longer a vaccine against paratyphoid.

The typhoid vaccine has been "cleaned up," and progress has been made on other new or better vaccines. A whole new clutch will appear within the next five years. The one that excites me most is the ETEC vaccine that should protect against the deviant of our normal bowel flora, which is responsible for the majority of cases of travelers' diarrhea (see page 3). Anyone traveling to a developing country has around a 50–50 chance of getting gyppy tummy, and many of us will welcome a vaccine that can be taken by mouth. The first ETEC vaccine should become available in 2001. And, no doubt, the next decade will bring capsules to protect us against bacilliary dysentery and many other possible causes of travelers' diarrhea.

The situation with poliomyelitis (polio) is changing, and it will be worth contacting a travel health clinic or the CDC to ask whether immunization is necessary for your destination. At the time of writing, the Americas had been declared free from the disease, but immunization (by bitter drops onto the tongue or on a sugar lump) was still recommended for much of the Old World.

An injectable cholera vaccine has been available for decades, but it gives a sore arm and it is rather ineffective. Furthermore, ordinary, well-nourished travelers are not at significant risk of disease from the cholera organism, and the World Health Organization revised the regulations controlling international travel and cholera cover. Now no reputable travel clinic recommends it, and immunization certificates should no longer be demanded at border posts. Unfortunately, unscrupulous border officials have been known to extort bribes to let travelers through without certificates, even though the certificate was not required. It is often a good idea to travel with lots of official-looking health documents; sometimes they impress officials enough to allow an untroubled passage. Recommendations about cholera immunization may change as more effective vaccines are developed or as disease patterns evolve. An oral vaccine (capsules) is available in Switzerland although it is not routinely dispensed there or in other European countries.

I visited a doctor in Kathmandu in the 1970s because I needed a cholera immunization before traveling from there through China. The doctor said, "I'll give you the vaccination certificate, but there's no need for the injection. The vaccine is useless."

◆

*Simon Howarth, then 20, volunteer engineer in East Nepal*

Perhaps the most useful antigen against fecal-oral disease of travelers is against Hepatitis A virus. It has been estimated that around 5 percent of all travelers to the developing world will suffer from this kind of hepatitis and, once infected, it can leave you ill and lethargic for weeks or months. A course protects fully for ten years. It is a must for those traveling "rough," especially in tropical Latin America or the Indian subcontinent (including Nepal). This vaccine supersedes the old gamma globulin serum which gave partial protection for a few months only.

As immunization becomes possible against more and more infectious diseases, vaccine combinations are being launched to reduce the number of injections before any trip. When the different components have different booster intervals (as with hepatitis A and B, and also the new hepatitis A and typhoid), immunization schedules become mind-bogglingly complex. Furthermore, travel clinic nurses complain such combinations take up too much precious refrigerator space, so it will be interesting to see whether they become widely available.

There are increasing concerns about the recrudescence of tuberculosis (TB) globally, and I am often asked about whether the Bacille Calmette-Guérin (BCG) intradermal immunization is useful and protective. It does offer some protection but mainly against the two serious forms of the disease (TB meningitis and miliary TB). Its efficacy is less good for the most common forms of TB. In addition, giving BCG makes the diagnosis of TB more difficult for doctors.

For the bloody menson—Take a herb called centynodum that is to say a hundred knots and boil this herb in water until it is soft and put your feet in it, not too deep but about to the middle of the foot for if you put your foot over the ankle bone it will constipate you so severely peradventure you shall never go to stool.

♦

*Unknown English author, possibly Dame Juliana Berners, circa 1480*

American doctors tend not to give BCG, while British doctors will often recommend it for travelers to developing countries. Go with the advice of your doctor at home.

# TABLE: IMMUNIZATIONS RECOMMENDED FOR MANY TRIPS TO DEVELOPING COUNTRIES

| Disease | Booster interval | Route of disease transmission | Notes |
|---|---|---|---|
| Tetanus | 10 years | Dirty wounds | Wise for travelers and nontravelers alike |
| Diphtheria | 10 years | Airborne | Especially for Eastern Europe and Western Asia |
| Polio | 10 years | Filth-to-mouth | Still necessary for trips to the Old World |
| Hepatitis A | 10 years | Filth-to-mouth | Especially for Central and South America and the Indian subcontinent |
| Typhoid | 1–3 years | Filth-to-mouth | Especially for Central and South America and the Indian subcontinent |
| ETEC diarrhea | ? | Filth-to-mouth | Coming soon |
| Cholera | - | Filth-to-mouth | Not recommended at present |
| Yellow Fever | 10 years | Mosquito (dusk and day biter) | For much of the tropical Americas and parts of Africa |

| Disease | Booster interval | Route of disease transmission | Notes |
| --- | --- | --- | --- |
| Meningococcus (bacterial meningitis and septicemia) | 3–5 years | Airborne | Especially for Africa in Northern Hemisphere winter months |
| Rabies | 3 years | Animal bites | Much of the developing world |
| Hepatitis B | About 5 years | Dirty hypodermic needles, and sex | Long-term expatriates, in case of substandard emergency medical treatment |
| Tuberculosis (TB) | Once only | Airborne | The BCG immunization tends to be given by British doctors but not in America or mainland Europe |
| Influenza | Annually | Airborne | For at-risk travelers: asthmatics, diabetics, seniors |
| Pneumococcus | Once only | Airborne | For at-risk travelers: with no spleen or sickle cell disease |
| Japanese encephalitis | 2–3 years | Mosquito (dusk and night biter) | Parts of rural Asia; for development workers mainly |

# Tips

➤ The filth-to-mouth diseases (diarrhea, dysentery, typhoid, Hepatitis A, etc.) are most prevalent in tropical Latin America and the Indian subcontinent, including Nepal and Bhutan. It is best to be fully immunized against all possible filth-to-mouth diseases if visiting these regions.

➤ At present vaccines are available against several filth-to-mouth diseases (typhoid, hepatitis A, and polio), and they are recommended for many journeys. However, new vaccines will soon emerge and it is worth seeking up-to-date information from a travel clinic or from the CDC on what is available and necessary.

➤ Allow plenty of time to organize your pre-trip immunizations—six weeks or more.

➤ Immunizations are worthwhile but do not protect you from all diseases, nor do they protect from the most common cause of death abroad: accidents.

➤ Finally, remember that immunization only protects against a tiny minority of travelers' health risks. To be sure to survive your trip:

- Remember that emergency services and health facilities may not be as good as at home; don't take risks.
- Think safe; foresee and forestall accidents.
- Play safe on any sexual encounters.
- Protect yourself from biting insects, especially from dusk until dawn.
- Fair-skinned adventurers should avoid excessive exposure to the sun, especially during the middle of the day. Skin cancer is increasing among white travelers.

I arrived in Madagascar in 1986 from Thailand via India and Kenya, and the health authorities in Antananarivo wanted to keep a close eye on my health. Maybe they thought I'd imported cholera from India and yellow fever from Nairobi. To make sure I reported to the Health Ministry, they confiscated my immunization certificates, and only reluctantly returned them the day before I left Madagascar.

◆

*Simon Howarth, 46, irrigation engineer, Cambridge, UK*

*Chapter 10*

# COPING WITHOUT PAPER
## TIME-HONORED METHODS FOR
## KEEPING CLEAN

Cleanliness is half of the Faith.

— *Koran*

*I*n cosmopolitan meeting places, like airports and universities, one can find evidence of others' difficulties in unfamiliar lavatories: footprints on the toilet seat betray a squatter struggling with our strange Western facilities. Local experts using their own familiar squat loos usually use water to clean themselves, and so their toilets are furnished with a tap or bucket for this and also to flush the toilet. Anal cleansing with water is an excellent and hygienic habit which most Westerners find quite revolting, yet citizens of warmer countries find our habit of using paper instead of water incomprehensibly uncivilized and dirty. Just think of all that unsightly used toilet paper! The River Cam that flows through Cambridge in England was once the city's sewer and, while on a tour of Trinity College, Queen Victoria asked "What are all those pieces of paper floating down the river?"

After living in Pakistan, I use water in the wilds. This has two advantages—you don't have to carry toilet paper and there's no messy paper left behind.

♦

*Phil Brabbs, 42, teacher trainer, Plzen, Czech Republic*

With great presence of mind her guide, Master of Trinity Dr. Whewell, replied "Those, ma'am, are notices that bathing is forbidden."

Yet toilet paper is a very recent invention. The first, Gayety's Medicated Paper, was produced (in England) in 1857 and came in flat packs. It was a product for the rich, and one that people were embarrassed to purchase; it was kept out of sight under the counter and euphemistically called curl papers. Toilet rolls appeared in 1928, and soft paper was introduced in 1932 but it was unpopular at first. As a child in the early 1930s in London, my mother tore up squares of newspaper to be left in the lavatory for bottom-wiping; it becomes softer and more absorbent, she says, if you crumple it before use.

Whatever you think of the technique, if you are traveling for months in a remote toilet-paper-free zone, anal cleansing with water is a skill worth mastering. Just think of the trees you are saving: in a lifetime, the average Westerner's toilet paper use consumes about twenty-two trees. The technique involves using *lots* of water; pour it directly onto your bottom

Cleaning oneself after defecation, throughout South Asia, involves…water…brought to the latrine site in a pottery, metal, or plastic vessel, called a *bodna* that has a spout, much like the spout of a teapot, and holds two to three liters of water. The use of this vessel is restricted to this one purpose. The…cleaning of the anal region occurs immediately after defecation. Water is poured from the *bodna* into a cupped left hand and then swiftly carried to the anal region. This process involves some skill and is taught to small children at an early age. After [that the left hand is] rubbed with soil…the individual pours water from the *bodna* onto the left hand for rinsing.

◆

Dr. Bilqis Hoque, et al., Journal of Tropical Medicine and Hygiene (1995)

to flush all the unpleasant stuff and then there is little need to use your fingers. In a warm climate washing like this is considerably more hygienic than using paper and will help reduce thrush and fungal infections around the groin: the damp area dries quickly without a towel. But one warning: it is extremely difficult to wash like this when on a conventional pedestal toilet. The usual result is that you will pour water all over your pants. I am now fairly comfortable with this technique although my left-handedness caused me some dilemmas at first. I wondered whether I should follow the local convention of reserving the left hand for the bum and the right for food: when traveling in Asia, it is good to be proficient at eating rice and sloppy vegetable curry without cutlery. At first I rinsed my bottom with my right hand and stuffed rice into my mouth with my left, until one dignified old Indian lady took me to one side. "Look, my dear...I don't mind, but here in India ortho-

In a remote village in Chin State, Myanmar (Burma), I was ushered to a toilet. My hostess must have decided that I could use some paper. Over the gap above the door she threw in a few sheets of thick white photocopy paper: not very pliable, not readily biodegradable. I folded it, shoved it in my handbag and used water.

♦

*Glenys Chandler, Ph.D., 55, community development specialist, Melbourne, Australia*

Best of both worlds: moisten toilet paper in water and then use it to clean yourself. Repeat if necessary. Pat dry with toilet paper only. In India and Nepal most people, after using the bathroom, do not use soap and water, but dirt from the ground to clean their hands, and then rinse their dirt-smeared hands with water. Dirty dishes too are "cleaned" with dirt or ash.

♦

*Rajendra S. Khadka, editor of* Travelers' Tales Nepal

dox people will be shocked if you eat using your left hand. You do know what we Indians do with our left hands, don't you?" Thereafter I washed my bottom with my sinister hand and was less than dextrous in conveying rice to my mouth with my clumsy right hand. In Pakistan I was told to be careful of holding out an outstretched hand when indicating how many items you want to buy in the market.

Apparently holding up a hand palm forward, fingers outstretched in a way you might when requesting five bananas is incredibly rude. To a Pakistani it says "you are the fifth son of the fifth wife" and Muslims are only allowed four wives. Making this gesture with the left hand further increases the insult to the recipient's ancestry.

Interestingly, although scouring the hands or plates with dirt or ash seems unhygienic, research in Dhaka published by Dr. Bilquis Hoque and colleagues (reported in *Journal of Tropical Medicine & Hygiene* 98-1995 and in *Public Health* 109-1995) has shown that cleaning (by scouring) the hands with mud or ash and plenty of water is bacteriologically fine: just as good as with soap. The scientists assessed the numbers of fecal bacteria remaining on hands after using different washing agents; mud, ash, and soap all achieved

In the early days of Nepalese tourism, the guest houses of Namche Bazaar had a certain reputation—or at least their loos did. I was last there in January 1983, when for several weeks the temperature hovered around freezing. By the middle of the month, frozen brown stalagmites had started to rise through the holes in the outside loos. Tales abounded of visitors doing battle with these burgeoning beasts; but to my enormous relief I found that my landlord had thoughtfully provided a small hammer.

♦

*John Pilkington, 50, explorer and author, Winchester, Hampshire, UK*

satisfactory levels of bacteriological cleanliness. It is a useful, cheap means for poor villagers to wash. People may prefer soap for cosmetic reasons, but the poor cannot afford such luxuries.

It is crucially important for travelers in less-hygienic regions to take special care in washing their hands before eating, and preferably after defecating. It is not always possible to find soap and running water in the place of easement, which is perhaps, why door handles of squalid toilets will be hopping with virulent microbes. Whatever washing agent is used, whether it is soap or mud or ash, it is the rubbing process that gets rid of microbes; rinsing with water alone does not produce effective cleaning. Similarly, campers can scour plates clean with mud, ash, or riverside moss, then rinse and dry them in the sun; this will make them clean enough and safe enough.

Traveling the back roads to Timbuktu, an occasional store may have a toilet roll lurking on the top shelf—retrieved by a rickety ladder and a storekeeper muttering "tourists" as he blows the thick layer of dust off. Failing this—and if dysentery strikes—you may have to say "When in Rome..." After three weeks of using your left hand for previously unimaginable tasks, it becomes easier, but you may need to carry extra water for your toilet ablutions.

♦

*Fran King, 37, trans-African cyclist and veterinary nurse, Hornchurch, Essex, UK*

Even the well-adapted adventurer might find herself in the great outdoors without paper and without water, so then what do you do? The Roman soldiers used sponges soaked in vinegar, while more refined citizens used wool soaked in perfume, and rich ladies used ostrich feathers. Excavations in English medieval cesspits (we English have the strangest hobbies) suggest that people then used various materials to wipe their bottoms: the poor used leaves, moss, or stones while moneyed people cut up their worn out clothes. And even today, in poor communities, practices are similar. Where water is short, people use leaves, dirt, or stones. If you too have to resort to using leaves, though, be careful what you use. Some leaves sting or irritate and others may harbor a noxious insect.

Ancient Romans revered two deities of the toilet: Crepitus was the god of the loo and Cloacina the goddess of the common sewer. Roman public lavatories, called *cloaca* in her honor, contained shrines where people made offerings to Cloacina. If such facilities were not immediately available, rich Romans would snap their fingers, and a slave would bring a special cloak and potty for immediate relief. A similar system was available to the public in Tudor Edinburgh. Men wandered the streets crying, "Wha wants me for a bawbee?" and for that fee (a bawbee is a coin worth three Scottish pennies)

Mobile toilets on tricycles can now be found in the city of Taiyuan, Shanxi province, China, where they are popular in crowded places like the railway station or public squares. Their designer, Xue Mingyuan, a former peasant farmer, said that the toilets are convenient for pedestrians and the floating population of migrant workers, who have difficulty finding a toilet in large cities. They are one-fourteenth the cost of a traditional free-standing toilet.

♦

*Found by Tim Burford in the* Guardian

In one town in India, the only loo available was a men's urinal and I was wearing dungarees. While struggling to "go" I looked up to find the windows crammed with peering faces. Traveling women shouldn't wear dungarees.

♦

*Dr. Ildiko Schuller, 38, pediatrician and mother, London, UK*

you would be provided with a bucket and a tentlike cloak. That is how a problem was solved in Britain. In parts of Southeast Asia (e.g., Indonesia) people believe—or at least act as if they believe—that they are invisible while they are "performing"—they aren't embarrassed if you aren't. Whereas in Nepal, people say, "The person witnessing someone shitting is more embarrassed than the shitter."

I had lived in Nepal several years before my Nepali language skills were good enough to dare ask the low-caste attendant in the Kathmandu airport lavatory about the facilities. In the main part of the Ladies, opposite the wash basins, were ceramic plates with a tiny drain hole. The attendant, amused by my ignorance, gathered the enormous folds of her sari around herself and squatted over one to demonstrate that it was a urinal: saris, *lungis*, and sarongs nicely preserve feminine modesty even while urinating in the public part of the lavatory; the trick is faciltiated by the absence of underwear. These Eastern-style facilities were only provided in the domestic terminal; apparently planners expect all international travelers to cope with Western toilets.

Your last piece of toilet paper. Fold it in quarters and tear off the corner so that you have made a small hole in the center of the square. Keep this small piece. Insert your left index finger through the hole wipe the mess off your bottom with the same finger, then wipe the mess off your finger by wrapping the toilet paper down around it as you slide it off. Remove remaining excreta from under your nail with the retained corner. Find some water to wash!

◆

*Paul Goodyer, 43, managing director of Nomad Travel Pharmacy, London, UK*

# Tips

➢ Wise travelers carry a small supply of toilet paper.

➢ Wet wipes can be useful, especially if you have a particularly messy diarrheal bowel action. They are also useful for superficially cleaning your hands if there is no water about, but be sure to wash with soap and water when you can.

➢ If traveling long term, learn how to clean up with water and no paper. If you are a novice in the technique I suggest fully removing the lower garments so that they don't get wet. Use lots of water and pour it straight onto the messy area with the jug or mug provided.

➢ In desert areas you may need to carry extra water for anal cleansing.

➢ Offering people things with your left hand will give offense in many cultures

On the *Sarimanok* sailing canoe we had no lavatory but hung with our posteriors over the sea. On the rare occasions when the sea was calm, we could sit on the paired outrigger supports. Sometimes the sea came up to dunk our bare bottoms, and Steve remarked while in motion "Hey, this is like going in a washing machine. It cleans you up lovely!"

◆

*Sally Crook, 47, nutritionist and author of* Distant Shores: By Traditional Canoe from Asia to Madagascar

Carry a small bottle of eucalyptus oil and a light cotton scarf when traveling. Then before entering that Third World toilet, just dab a little of the oil onto the scarf and pull the scarf up over your mouth and nose; this helps disguise the odors that make you dry-retch.

◆

*Kellie Primmer, 29, travel consultant, Victoria, Australia*

since the left hand is reserved for anal cleansing. Experts keep their left hand for the anus and their right for eating and shaking hands. Left-handed travelers may cause unintended offense by handing people things with their left hand.

➢ Take care what you use to wipe your bottom; some leaves sting, others will cause irritation. Avoid wiping your bottom on any "hairy" leaves. These will definitely cause you grief.

➢ Scrunching up hard paper makes it slightly more soft and absorbent and better for wiping your bottom.

➢ Those with sensitive noses should travel with some strong-smelling potion to disguise those foul loo stinks. Carry matches.

---

All kinds of toilet accessories are available in Japan including antiseptic wipes, seat covers, and pocket-size sprays in case you leave a nasty smell.
Toilets come in four grades:

Traditional—a basic urinal set in the floor, paper usually not provided

Basic— similar to the loos we know at home

Deluxe—this is the most common; it has a heated seat

Super Deluxe or "Full Service"—with lots of buttons and dials that I've never dared use, but one makes the sound of a flushing toilet, and so disguises any embarrassing sounds you make. The plumbing is designed so that the water you wash your hands with is used to flush away your "doings."

◆

*Jo Surtees, 29, wandering English teacher, Iwate-ken, Japan*

## Chapter 11

# CAN IT BE WORMS?

## AVOIDING THEM

Travel broadens the mind and
loosens the bowels.

— *Anonymous*

———

$\mathcal{I}$'d been back from India a few months and was sitting on the loo. The long overland trip had left my bowels somewhat friskier than before the trip, but the symptoms were settling. That day though, I was aware of a strange sensation, and looked between my legs to see a worm dangling from my anus. Thankfully it had died of old age. It wasn't moving. My interest in parasitology overcame my revulsion, and I recovered the worm. It was superficially similar to an earthworm, pinkish-white, about twelve inches long: *Ascaris lumbricoides*. This is probably the most common parasite of humans globally. It is a tremendously successful species because its microscopic eggs are incredibly resistant to inhospitable environments; it can blow around in the wind, settle on food, and if you eat this food unwashed or uncooked, this roundworm can set up home inside you. They are utterly revolting but really rather harmless. They have no hooks or suckers and spend their short lives (twelve to eighteen months) desperately swimming upstream within the intestine trying to avoid leaving with your bowel movements. Travelers rarely acquire more than one or two, whereas children of the developing world can end up with 100 or more inside them when they can clog the gut and cause malnutrition or even death. If you pass one, get a stool sample examined under the microscope to see if there are any more, and take treatment if necessary.

*Ascaris* roundworms and the similar, smaller *Trichuris* whipworms are acquired from contaminated food, but there are a couple of worms that have evolved cleverer means of gaining access to our bodies. These are first deposited in the soil in the stool of someone with the worms, and then the worm eggs hatch and can penetrate the skin of your feet if you happen to walk barefoot in a contaminated place. They cause a little patch of irritation at the site of penetration and then ride in the bloodstream, eventually setting up home in the gut. Hookworm and *Strongyloides* are the two worms entering by this route. Hookworm rarely colonizes travelers in sufficient numbers to cause symptoms or problems, and infestations will often fade out without people knowing they have carried a few unwelcome hitchhikers. *Strongyloides* can cause some unpleasant illnesses however. Nick Garbutt, wildlife photographer and author, told me about one such infestation:

> For the third morning running, I woke up feeling as though my body had been through a mangle—muscles I didn't realize I possessed ached. The cold, damp rain forest floor was to blame. But why did I have technicolor sores covering my feet, the itchy rash around my middle, and dramatic rumblings in my gut? Things got worse when I got home from Madagascar: stomach rumbles became severe abdominal pain, intestinal volcanoes erupted frequently, producing farts straight from Satan's bottom, and life beyond a stone's throw from a toilet ceased. At the Infectious Disease Unit in Sheffield I was the center of much interest. "Looks like strongyloidiasis,"

they said and took me up to the lab to look down the microscope at the culprit: hundreds of them, *Strongyloides stercoralis*, microscopic worms that invade people but are unique among human parasites in being able to survive in soil for several generations. They burrow through the skin of the feet and ride around in the blood causing irritating rashes. The parasite can then maintain itself for thirty years without new infections from the environment. Fortunately, a short course of horse pills made visits to the loo less frequent, and eating became a pleasure again, although rashes and skin sores continued for two more months.

The geography worm or *larva migrans* is a different, less noxious species that causes a very itchy, dry, flaky, red track usually on the feet or buttocks, wherever the skin has been in contact with ground contaminated with dog (or cat) feces. Travelers get it after walking barefoot or sitting on contaminated beaches. The Caribbean and Sri Lanka are two places to catch it. The dog (or cat) hookworm larva that causes the problem penetrates the skin, then wanders in vain looking for some dog flesh in which to set up home. It sadly roams the skin for many weeks, until it finally dies unfulfilled. The head

We rented an annex room in Goa. Our toilet (a squatter with a bucket of water to flush it) was fifty yards away. I had dysentery and while making frequent, rushed trips to the bottom of the garden, I wondered how the toilet was kept so clean. One particularly bad day, after many fifty-yard waddles, I found my answer—Todo, the family pig, used toilet offerings as a dietary supplement.

◆

*Ian Carter, 31, climber, London, UK*

of the track advances a few millimeters each day; the map-like pattern it leaves explains why it is also called the geography worm. The worm will do you no harm, but you will probably want to be rid of it because of the irritation it causes. Treatment can be by freezing the head of the worm with liquid carbon dioxide or liquid nitrogen, or with tablets.

Most worms have rather complex life cycles and often spend part of their existence in another species. The tapeworms are perhaps the best known of these, and many people are aware that in less-hygienic environments it is wise to eat any meat well done. Rare steaks can give you beef tapeworm, and rare pork or wild boar steaks may harbor pork tapeworm. The beef tapeworm can reach a length of forty-nine feet yet the symptom that may make you aware of the presence of a tapeworm is that worm segments that are actually sacks of eggs, come out of the anus. These are mobile and look themselves like tiny worms. This is alarming but is unlikely to harm your health; treatment is straightforward.

An anxious expatriate mother in Kathmandu asked my advice. "My cook has roundworms. What can I do? Will we all get infested?"

I explained that roundworm eggs need a period of maturation in soil before they become infective so a cook will not pass them on via the food she prepares. The cook was treated and looked healthier and happier subsequently, and the expatriate family stayed worm-free.

♦

JW-H

Worms are not only a hazard of tropical trips. Like tapeworms, *Trichinella* are worms that are also acquired from eating inadequately cooked pork, and these are by no means confined to the tropics. If you eat raw or undercooked polar bear, walrus, or wild boar in the Arctic you can acquire trichinosis.

Terrific itching around the anus, especially at night, may also be a sign of a worm infestation. This is the main symptom of threadworm or pinworm. These are tiny and are ubiquitous wherever there are children, both in the developed and less developed world. Again, treatment is straightforward, although it is also necessary to combine medical treatment with meticulous personal hygiene.

The guinea or Medina worm (*Dracunculus*) is an unpleasant infestation that is caught by swallowing miniscule freshwater "fleas." Drinking only boiled, filtered, or strained water will protect you. It is rapidly nearing extinction throughout much of its range: equatorial Africa, eastern India, Pakistan, southwest Saudi Arabia, and southern Iraq. Don't worry about it.

## *Tips*

➢ Avoid walking barefoot, even on the beach. Wearing shoes helps avoid geography worm, hookworm, as well as injuries from coral and sea urchin spines entering the feet.

➢ Excruciating itching around the anus especially at night is likely to be an infestation of threadworm, *Enterobius vermicularis*. Medicines clear this quickly but be sure

In two and a half months of cycling alone across China in 1985, I never got sick once, despite always eating at filthy-looking roadside noodle stalls. Meanwhile many travelers who ate in hotels ended up with serious gut problems. I attribute this to the fact that the raw ingredients were cooked in front of me and served within minutes of my order, whereas food in government-run hotels sat around on hot plates for ages. My worst problem was a constantly burned mouth.

◆

*Catherine Hopper, 37, cycling Buddhist, Manchester, UK*

while taking treatment that you keep your fingernails cut short and wash meticulously after going to the toilet otherwise you will reinfect yourself and others.

➤ When in less-hygienic environments, steaks and other meats should be freshly cooked and eaten well-done to avoid tapeworms and other gastrointestinal troubles. Meat harboring tapeworm cysts is "measly"—it looks white-speckled.

➤ Beef tapeworm infests not only cows but also buffaloes and yaks, and pork tapeworm can infest dogs.

➤ A selection of unpleasant flukes are acquired from eating raw or lightly cooked fish and shellfish or water plants (like watercress) which have been contaminated with excrement.

➤ Long-term travelers do not need to take regular courses of worm medicines as some people believe. Most worms do little harm and are usually present in modest numbers.

Fast bowler at the Oval, fresh back in England from an Indian tour, running up to bowl and, suddenly caught short, kept on down the wicket, off the field and into the pavilion.

♦

*Joseph Wilson, 79, retired school master, Surrey, England*

## Chapter 12

# BAD BEASTS
## SNAKES AND SPIDERS AND
## LEECHES, OH MY!

Zookeeper Friedrich Riesfedt dosed his constipated elephant twenty-
two times with laxatives as well as feeding him figs and prunes.
Finally, while Riesfedt was administering an olive oil enema, the
elephant explosively unloaded 200 pounds of excrement, knocked
the keeper unconscious and he suffocated beneath the pile.

— *Reported in* Himal *magazine, Kathmandu, November 1998*

———

*B*athrooms and toilets are cool, damp, and often gloomy.
Outside facilities seem especially attractive refuges for a
range of beasts. But what? Is this the place you'll meet
ticks, leeches, and venomous snakes? Occasionally an outside
loo might harbor a snake, but more likely the animals that
surprise you will be smaller: responsible for unnerving scut-
tling noises and only scary until you find out it was a panicking
mouse or cockroach. Various creatures wander inside searching
for pickings, while field wasps and even bees nest in some outside loos. I staggered out one morning up at 11,500 feet in the
Helambu region of Nepal. The scene was glorious: frost on the
ground; rhododendrons in pink, lilac, and white growing
around a dry-stone long-drop. I squatted to perform and
noticed large bees dodging my stream of urine; they were coming up to investigate the source of pollution of their nest site.
I'd left calmly (flailing about encourages them to attack in
force) and the lodge owner persuaded the bees to move house

by dropping some flaming rags soaked in kerosene into the pit. In a simple long-drop you should be able to see any hazardous beasts, but toilet seats might hide something unexpected. In the southern United States, venomous brown spiders (*Loxosceles spp.*) may set up home under the seat of an outside toilet. Occasionally they bite male organs that intrude on the spider's territory. Australian outside lavatories (*dunnies*) carry similar health warnings.

I was the first person that morning to use the hole-in-the-ground bush toilet at our campsite in Tarangire National Park, Tanzania. As I started to relieve myself, a very shocked and wet bat flew out of the hole straight into my face.

♦

*Sean Moore, 34,*
*marketing manager,*
*Northolt, Middlesex, UK*

In warm climates in the spring, there are often population explosions of hairy caterpillars; they seem to get everywhere. The "fur" of these animals is actually thousands of minute hypodermics packed with histamines and other irritant chemicals. Check that there are none on the toilet paper before using it, and check your clothes when you get dressed in the morning.

It is astonishing just where small creatures get to. I was running mobile medical clinics in Sri Lanka where mothers complained that when their children defecated, beetles flew out of the freshly deposited stool. I

Nature called in the middle of the night in India and I crept out to the shack in the courtyard. I was sitting there when—midstream—something cold and wet attacked my private parts. Shrieking I jumped up. I shook as I turned my flashlight toward the toilet. Inside were half a dozen green frogs.

♦

*Margaret Strong, Exeter,*
*Devon, UK*

didn't believe these tales at first, but it transpired that certain dung beetles lay their eggs just within the anus of small children, the eggs hatch, the beetle larvae feast lavishly—and harmlessly—and then are liberated when the child "goes."

Groping about in the dark, or reaching into niches where you cannot see may be unwise. A scorpion in Madagascar stung me when I was rummaging blindly in the corner of my rucksack. Scorpions lurk in confined places and are often disturbed by the unwary, and there are dangerous species in North Africa and the Middle East, Mexico and Arizona, and in South India; elsewhere their sting is unpleasant but not deadly. But wherever you are out of doors, use your flashlight at night. Come evening, tropical toilets and outside bathrooms are often alive with hungry mosquitoes—this is not a good time for a visit, unless you have had the forethought to spray the smallest room with insecticide beforehand or have covered yourself with insect repellent.

On Tioman Island off the east coast of Malaysia, we had to use a water-filled squat loo where lived a gecko. He waited with his body under the water, front feet firmly stuck to the sides of the ceramic pan, head held high, neck stretched out, always ready to receive our humble droppings.

◆

*Mary Kenny, 36, editor and mother, Delhi, India*

Creatures find both showers and bathrooms attractive. In a forest reserve in Sri Lanka the only available lights were hurricane lamps. With the unearthly jungle sounds, the flickering weird shadows were a little unnerving. I stripped off to shower when something cold and clammy hit and stuck to my backside. I jumped, then realized it was only a tree frog confused by the light. The walls were covered in them. They were all trying to stay stuck high on the tiled walls, but each was slowly sliding down to the floor. It's strange how, in an unfamiliar environment and especially in poor lighting, the imagination runs riot and even harmless little animals can scare.

There can be surprising finds in latrine pits. When we went to use the open, shallow latrine pit at our base camp in the forest at Ankarana, we often disturbed attractive Madagascar ring-tailed mongooses, *Galidia elegans*.

Little red-backed spiders of Australia are said to be venomous and they lurk under toilet seats. When we were in the Outback we were warned to rattle seats before using the toilet.

♦

*Barbara Ikin, 47, Swiss development worker, Maputo, Mozambique*

They did not seem so *elegant* when we'd see one emerging from the pit, a half-eaten maggot still protruding from its mouth. They were responsible for some unnerving nocturnal rustlings on occasion. Pigs and dogs, too, find excreta delicious and in many countries that lack proper sewerage systems, they provide that disposal service.

Wildlife—both large and small—is attracted to our food, and some species can be a terrific nuisance. In some locations ants are an enormous pest. If the sugar is infested, put it into the tea strainer (rather than the cup) and then pour the milk and tea or coffee through the sugar. Thus the ants are sieved from the sugar, leaving an interesting, harmless formic acid piquancy to the beverage. Larger animal thieves come (theoretically at

At George Adamson's camp at Kora National Reserve (Kenya) the toilet was an elephant jawbone. This lower jawbone when turned upside down is a perfect toilet seat!

♦

*Shailesh Chandaria, 43, tour operator, Nairobi, Kenya*

least) with some increased health risks. Pariah kites living close to the plush international hotels of Karachi learned to take chicken portions from the hands of guests reclining by the pool, and Sri Lankan hotel crows loved snatching beakfuls of sugar from tea trays. Birds can carry salmonella, which might cause gastroenteritis, or at least it might if they leave you anything to eat! And if a dog licks a plate or interferes with your food, you risk *Giardia* and also a nasty parasitic infection called hydatid disease. It is probably best to avoid food that has been shared with birds or larger animals, particularly if they are scavengers by nature.

## *Tips*

➢ Nocturnal wanderers in bush or jungle should wear stout shoes and long pants.

➢ Take a flashlight when seeking relief in the bush or Outback after dark.

➢ Most toilet encounters are with harmless creatures—they're more terrified of you than you need be of them. Pigs or dogs may follow you hoping for something you produce, but these are easily put to flight.

On the Silk Route between Beijing and Islamabad, taking your trowel into the wilds proved the best toilet. The Chinese lavatories stank—all except one. Here, as each person finished, the local dogs rushed in and removed everything.

◆

*Julie Eames, 50, retired salesperson, Southampton, UK*

➢ Especially in outside toilets in the tropics, check before you sit or squat.

➢ Just make sure there are no hairy caterpillars or other

little meanies on the toilet paper before you use it.

➤ Never put your hand where you cannot see lurking dangers.

➤ A headlamp is very useful when "going" in a dark place; it leaves your hands free for stopping clothes from falling into the mess, etc.

➤ The most dangerous creature that you are likely to encounter in a tropical toilet is the mosquito. If you are in a region where mosquito-borne disease is a risk, avoid visits at dusk to primitive toilets or bathrooms unless you are wearing long clothes and repellent. Try to time your evening shower for a little before dusk.

➤ Old World rain forests and also Asian forests during the monsoon are places to pick up leeches. They are harmless but revolting, their bites bleed for hours, and these easily become infected in hot, humid climates. Apply a DEET-based insect repellent to your ankles or on your shoes when venturing into leech country. This will keep them off. Or get them off with a dab of salt or tobacco.

At work in Gede, Kenya, the toilet is a long-drop crowned by a box with a seat on it. When flies are disturbed in the depths they try to leave by the only available exit, collide with my bared anatomy, and end up, stunned, in my pants. Strange buzzing sounds sometimes come from below my belt. In Kenya, public toilets are rare, but even when found they may not be the place you want to drop your pants: they are often full of hungry mosquitoes.

◆

*Sally Crook, 47, British entomologist and community development advisor, Watamu, Kenya*

➤ While some travelers rely on alternative remedies, prophylaxis, and cures, I would counsel using only conventional medicines and effective chemical repellents in protecting yourself from death from malaria. The best repellents are DEET-based, and those based on natural oils are not effective enough against rampant African malarious mosquitoes.

In Kerala, India, I got "the call" and rushed into the forest. Later I felt something cold on my ankle. Our driver said, "Don't worry, Madam, it is not dangerous; it is only leech," as he squashed it and my blood oozed out onto the road. Later still I discovered that my trouser leg was soaked with blood. Panicking I asked the driver to look away while I disrobed to investigate. There was only one bite hole just behind my knee.

◆

*Linda Davis, 55, recently qualified mahout, Haslemere, Surrey, UK*

# Chapter 13

## GOING OUTSIDE
### TAKING CARE OF NATURAL
### ACTS IN NATURE

...when thou wilt ease thyself abroad, thou shalt dig,
and shalt turn back and cover that
which cometh from thee.

— *Deuteronomy 23:13*

———

*O*ut in the wilds, enjoying that invigorating feeling of being away from people, you take a deep breath and that smell reaches your nostrils; that smell or a vision of a brown deposit—or worse—the realization you've just stepped in it. It just spoils your moment, your day. But maybe the poor unfortunate who left the deposit had nowhere else to "go." It's a problem, isn't it? Or is it? Actually it is not so difficult to dispose of your offerings responsibly. Ideally your turd should be buried in the top six to eight inches of organic soil, and covered with six inches of dirt; in this way your offering will be hygienically and efficiently absorbed into the nutrient cycle, and it is buried deep enough to discourage retrieval by scavengers. Animals may investigate deposits that are left above ground or shallowly buried, some will eat it, and badgers and dogs even like rolling in the stuff. A trowel or ice ax will assist you in conscientious burial. Hikers who are caught short can use their boot heel to excavate a bit of a hole. Otherwise in most environments it is possible to scrape away a bit of a depression in the dirt with your shoe. Then, bowels moved, you can burn the toilet paper (but beware of causing a forest fire) and then scuff some dirt over the mess to disguise it, or sprinkle leaf litter over it. Contact with soil and leaf litter speed decomposition, and so Kathleen Meyer, author of *How to Shit in the Woods*, suggests stirring your turd with a stick to mix it with some dirt. You could pick up a rock, crap, then replace the rock, but the next person might get an unpleasant surprise if they try the same trick, and actually squashing excrement under a rock slows nature's disposal system. Why not use a rock to excavate a shallow latrine hole? Or better still, make sure you "go" in the morning before leaving your campsite, where facilities may be provided or are easier to improvise.

In some parts of North America, walkers and climbers are encouraged, and sometimes required, to carry out all their excrement from a wilderness area. Lack of suitable containers, biodegradable bags, and disposal facilities in Europe make this option fraught with practical problems, so that it is not currently recommended. At present, burial is the recommended method. If in snow, dig down to soil. If there is no soil, the technique suggested by Meyer, is to find a discreet place, spread the feces thinly using a trowel or flat rock, then cover—if you can—with a sprinkle of soil leaf litter or vegetation.

On our way to a new clinic, I needed a pee and asked the driver to stop. I walked off toward a small group of trees to hide behind them. Suddenly my Cambodian colleague came running after me waving his arms. "You can't go there! That's just the kind of place for a land mine." What could I do? Bouff! I just pulled down my pants and pissed on the road. Everyone could see but I didn't care. What else could I do?

◆

*Veronique McConnell, 37, nurse just after Cambodian war, France*

Otherwise she suggests smearing an eighth of an inch- (three-millimeter) thin layer on a rock like frosting (icing) on a cake. Spreading thinly speeds and assists the natural breakdown of the excrement, and if exposed to sunlight, the ultraviolet rays and also the drying process inactivates many nasty microbes; this latter idea can be used in mountain or desert regions, but beware of contaminating very fragile ecosystems. These options are rather unaesthetic too, yet dealing with your own products is so much better than being faced with other peoples' and is far preferable to the selfish drop-and-run technique practiced by so many. This is particularly noticeable in the Himalayas where my children have imported others' excreta into our tent!

Remember that a stream may be someone else's water supply so never "go" into water, but defecate at least thirty yards from any streams and rivers, and downstream of any settlement. When camping, take your own drinking water uphill from your site and defecate downhill. Although urine is less harmful than stools, try to be responsible about where you pee too. Avoid urinating at the foot of crags, in cave entrances, or behind buildings. And "go" at least 50 yards from paths and 200 yards from climbing huts, refuges, or other buildings.

Running a temporary clinic in western Madagascar, we resorted to using the cotton fields as a latrine. But although we always tried to wait until darkness fell, our bottoms shone like beacons in the moonlight. Here was another disadvantage of being white: our Malagasy colleagues could "go" unobserved.

◆

*Dr. Anne Denning, 37,
ophthalmic surgeon,
Bournemouth, UK*

When traveling by vehicle, there is often less choice in where we can "go." Taking the bus from Antananarivo to Fort Dauphin in Madagascar, I recall joining a line of women squatting behind a wall, a trickle of urine emerging from beneath the skirt of each woman. We stayed the night in a very basic *hotely*; the toilet there was a choice of a rather overfull slop bucket on the balcony overlooking the main street, a squat toilet which was blocked and seething with maggots, or "the bush." My flashlight was unreliable, and the "bush" comprised unpleasant, spiky thorn bushes so I was relieved to be able to teeter over the slop bucket in the privacy of darkness. I wonder what happened to the bucket; in the Hebrides a hundred years ago, chamber pots were emptied into a communal storage barrel so that Harris tweed could be soaked in urine to condition the cloth.

In rural north India, people will say that they are going to the *maidan*—literally an open space or field—when they need to go for a shit.

♦

*Rajendra S. Khadka, editor of* Travelers' Tales Nepal

Going outside for relief can have its hazards, even for locals. In India, space is at such a premium that the roadside is one of the few places people can squat. They venture out after dark and are hit by speeding cars. In Nepal, women are rendered night-blind by poor nutrition and the demands of pregnancy.

A headlamp is especially useful when relieving oneself in unusual places, much easier than gripping a flashlight in one's teeth—just turn it off before exposing oneself.

♦

*Jean Sinclair, 33, nurse, biologist, and expeditionary, Cambridge, UK*

Thus pregnant women there have almost double the risk of accidental death than nonpregnant women who can see at night, because they often fall off some dangerous ledge while out after dark opening their bowels. It is worth trying to avoid those unscheduled night calls, and if you do need to go outside make sure you carry a good functioning flashlight or headlamp.

Many predators, including snakes, scorpions, and giant centipedes, are nocturnal and you could encounter one in your nighttime perambulations. They also have the unfortunate habit of curling up in shoes and clothing and get upset when you, the owner, attempt to get dressed before a nocturnal outing. Check before you dress then and put on stout shoes and long pants to help protect you from these creatures. Be aware though, that few animals want to fight, so if you don't creep up on them but announce your arrival by stomping clumsily and noisily, you will be most unlikely to meet anything nasty. The light makes you visible as well as allowing you to sidestep hazards of the night. Some years ago my husband took me on a miserable trek in the monsoon rains. At the road head in East Nepal, we found spaces in a squalid second floor dormitory. I needed a pee in the night. It

My bladder was about to burst. Three of us were wedged into a second floor room with the only exit a creaky door just beyond my snoring companions. Past that was a precipitous staircase to the room where four generations of the family were sleeping, and beyond them lay doors bolted for the night. It was pitch-dark and I knew I'd never make it outside without waking the entire household and possibly killing myself in a tumble. My only recourse was the window by my cot that opened to the tile roof. I peed a torrent into the Himalayan night and have never felt such relief, realizing only afterward that someone may have been sleeping on the porch below.

♦

*Larry Habegger, 47,*
*writer and editor,*
*San Francisco, California*

was wet and windy so the candle went out several times as I scrambled down the steep outside steps to the toilet shack. I managed my pee by lighting more matches, but as I headed back inside, a drunk pissed off the balcony all over me. If only my flashlight had been working.

Several women travelers have told me that they reduce the amount that they drink if there are no "civilized" toilets available so that they don't *need* to pass water as often. I can understand the reasoning behind this but, especially in hot climates, this is a dangerous strategy. Reducing fluid intake will increase the chances of heat stroke and urinary tract infections; it may also lead to kidney stones. Everyone needs to produce three good-volume urinations a day, toilet or no toilet.

## *Tips*

➢ When hiking in toilet-free zones, check what you are expected to do with your excreta; some North American parks provide trowels or suitable bags as well as disposal sites.

➢ Self-composting dry toilets have been built in a few remote locations. Carefully follow the instructions on how to use it so that it continues to function after your visit.

➢ Remember that in many developing regions people "go" at night; the dark offers privacy so if there are no

Smart male trekkers in Nepal sleep with an empty plastic jar with a wide mouth. If the need arises at night, they piss into the jar and thereby avoid unwanted nocturnal encounters.

◆

*Rajendra S. Khadka, editor of* Travelers' Tales Nepal

facilities follow suit, but make sure you take a reliable flashlight. The light will help you avoid treading in others' deposits, and you can check the location for safety, too.

➤ If there are no en suite toilet facilities or the electricity supply is unreliable, make sure your flashlight is handy when you settle down to sleep for the night. Otherwise you might have trouble locating the loo later.

➤ When venturing into the bush or jungle for relief, wear stout shoes and long pants; this will protect you from scorpion stings and snakebite as well as thorn scratches and stubbed toes.

➤ Get dressed when you venture outside for relief after dark. If you have an accident or bump into someone, you will avoid embarrassment, and it also should reduce the chances of being bitten by mosquitoes.

➤ When "going" outside and you think others are around, whistling or singing will

I needed a shit in the middle of the night at our forest base camp at Ankarana, Madagascar. As I walked back, my feeble penlight stopped working and I was lost. I didn't have much on so I was loath to shout for help. I was just contemplating waiting for four hours until dawn broke, when Jean-Elie let out an enormous snore to guide me safely back to my hammock.

◆

*Dr. Anne Denning, 37, ophthalmic surgeon, Bournemouth, UK*

Beware of what you squat over especially at night: I have been unpleasantly surprised by fire ants in Bali, by thistles and stinging nettles in Ireland, and by sand fleas in Peru.

◆

*Anne Peniston, 46, international public health worker, Nepal*

warn people of your whereabouts; in Asia the locals will understand—they may think you are scared of ghosts.

➤ Rustlings and scuttlings sound louder at night; shining your flashlight toward some nocturnal monster will reveal itself as a chicken, cat, mouse, or some-such small harmless wanderer.

➤ In some regions you may encounter half-wild dogs; if they threaten you, stoop down as if to pick up a stone. This will put most dogs to flight. Carrying a stout walking stick is an additional protection against pariah dogs.

➤ Burning used toilet paper will reduce pollution and unsightly litter. Most responsible travelers will burn that which will burn and then bury everything. Methane gas is explosive, but this should only be a risk in confined, unventilated spaces.

➤ Don't "hang on" to bladder or bowel contents longer than feels comfortable, and don't restrict the amount you drink in order to avoid peeing; these are unhealthy practices.

➤ For females, expeditionary Jean Sinclair adds, a wide-mouthed can, such as Mornflakes porridge oats, which

----- ★ ★ -----

On a six-month overland tour of Africa we were told we must burn all used toilet paper. After a few drinks, Lucie visited the toilet tent. As the rest of us relaxed under the stars, there was a loud explosion and we turned to see the toilet tent in flames. Lucie, in setting fire to her toilet paper had ignited methane gas. She was all right but in her panic had left her pants in the inferno.

◆

*Anthea Iva, 28, adventure travel consultant, Victoria, Australia*

comes with a plastic lid, works well, provided you have been skillful with your can opener to produce a smooth edge. If women want to keep clear of a messy toilet, have difficulties squatting over a squatty, or can't hover over an airline toilet during turbulence, they may want to invest in a Whizzy, a cunning, foldable, disposable, gutterlike device that allows women to pee standing. They are available from New Angle Products, Box 25641, Chicago, IL 60625.

➤ At high altitude, temperatures plummet at night and going outside for a pee is a chilling experience. It can also be hazardous since you may slip on ice even inside the toilet; this might be squelchy.

➤ Some trekkers and mountaineers take acetazolamide (Diamox) capsules to speed acclimatization and reduce high-altitude insomnia; this medicine is a mild diuretic (stimulator of urine produc-

In rural Bangladesh, there are millions of people, little cover, and locals find foreigners fascinating. It is impossible, therefore, for women to relieve themselves outdoors in privacy. We traveled with three large cheap black Chinese umbrellas to hide behind when I needed to go.

◆

*Barbara Ikin, 47, development adviser, Mozambique*

When "going" outside in the Antarctic, excavate a hole and then sit on the spade for a comfortable shit, but beware, at subzero temperatures you will stick to a metal handle. Choose a wooden-handled spade.

◆

*Steve Colwell, 32, meteorologist, British Antarctic Survey, Cambridge, UK*

tion) so take them in the morning otherwise you will be awakened by your bladder in the night.

➤ Reindeer have a passion for human urine and so are easily tamed, ridden, and harnessed: watch where you pee in Lapland.

➤ When relieving yourself outdoors, think beyond preserving your modesty and avoid places where others might want to loiter or rest. Bury your excreta six inches deep if you can.

Middle of the Bering Strait, heaving seas, strong winds, and icebergs, ten hours out from Cape Prince of Wales, paddling single-seat kayaks. The toilet procedure was for two people to raft together. Robert then held my kayak while I unzipped my dry suit and carefully pushed a beaker down between my legs. Started to pee and when my thumb became warm I knew it was about to overflow. Now the tricky bit of extracting the beaker through a very tight dry suit without spilling it, trusting Robert not to let the kayak go.

◆

*Trevor Potts, 49, adventurer, Argyll, Scotland*

*Chapter 14*

# BATHING

## HAZARDS AND TECHNIQUES IN
## UNUSUAL CIRCUMSTANCES

Wading in, as the hanging mist over the river began to lighten and
lift…. I swam a little way off, into an upstream eddy by the bank,
and there, luckily, all alone I learned the most important lesson for
tranquil conduct of life in the jungle: never, ever, shit in a whirlpool.

— *Redmond O'Hanlon,* Into the Heart of Borneo

———

*H*ow safe is bathing outdoors? It is hard to imagine anything more appealing and natural than bathing in
some warm, natural body of water somewhere. But is
it risky? I've swum in a wonderfully private subterranean river
in Madagascar. I've bathed in fast-moving Amazonian waters
but, with all the tales I'd heard about piranhas, I was on edge
and when toothless fish came nibbling at my stomach, my
imagination invented man-eating beasts. It seems to have been
the hyperbolic accounts published by Theodore Roosevelt that
are the basis of the fearsome reputation of the piranha: there
are no reliable accounts of human deaths due to these fish.
Authenticated accounts are also wanting of damage done by the
mysterious candiru fish that is said to lodge itself inside swimmers' urethras. Travelers' folklore has it that if the victim is
male, the only treatment is penile amputation. The candiru is a
parasite that prefers to settle down inside the gills of other fish.

The biggest real threat from freshwater bathing is
drowning—and losing the soap. There are a few nasty aquatic

animals that may cause some grief but the chances of meeting any are slim. Tropical South American rivers can harbor stingrays which can cause exceedingly nasty injuries, but the reputations of many other dangerous beasts seem exaggerated. In Africa, crocodiles and hippos are dangerous. There is a river in western Madagascar called Tsiribihina that means, "Where you mustn't swim." Why? Because Nile crocodiles will probably eat you. Take local advice before bathing outdoors. The risks of upsetting a large animal are small, yet there are some real hazards. Bathing outdoors in much of Africa can put you at risk of schistosomiasis (also known as bilharzia). This parasite spends part of its life in freshwater snails and part in larger animals such as humans. People suffering from bilharzia pass eggs in their urine or feces, and if these enter suitable, well-oxygenated freshwater, they will hatch out and swim off in search of a snail to infest. Here the parasite multiplies then goes out into a free-swimming stage again, but in this form the miniscule worm is capable of

In the Apo Kayan, far in the north of East Kalimantan, villagers had delineated three sections of the river for different uses. The most upstream section was for fetching drinking water, next there was the bathing and washing area, whilst the section farthest downstream was for defecating. There is an art to crapping in the river. Wear a sarong rather than shorts or skirt and underwear. Firstly, move in far enough from the bank where the water is actually flowing (near the bank it is often very slow moving indeed) or you will find yourself using your hands to stir up the water to get your turd to travel away. Secondly, face upstream. It is disconcerting to be confronted with one's own emission as it flows past.

♦

*Glenys Chandler, Ph.D., 55, community development specialist, Melbourne, Australia*

digesting its way through the flesh of anyone who happens to be paddling or bathing. This causes "swimmers itch" as the worm penetrates the skin and then the parasite rides in the bloodstream until eventually it sets up home in bladder (*Schistosoma haematobium*) or bowel (*Schistosoma mansoni*), where it settles down to producing millions of eggs. Travelers are infected when swimming or paddling in waters contaminated with human waste, which usually means that the victim has paddled or swum within 200 yards of a village or point where people are using water— for washing clothes perhaps, or where village children romp. Infected travelers tend to get ill with a fever, and once alerted to this infection, there is a very effective cure in the drug praziquantel. A blood test done *more* than six weeks after last possible exposure to the parasite, and preferably within twelve weeks of possible infection, will establish the diagnosis. The highest-risk geographical regions are the great lakes of the east African Rift Valley, but the infection can be acquired from many freshwater lakes, streams, and slow-moving rivers where there is waterweed for the snails to feed on. There are foci in the Middle East, and in the tropical Americas (northeast Brazil, the Guianas, Surinam, Venezuela, and some Caribbean islands).

The species that occur in Africa and the Middle East

Disposal of sanitary products and condoms may be a problem for travelers. These should not be flushed down any toilet anywhere. The UK has a "Bag It and Bin It" campaign, supported by water companies, and sanitary product and condom manufacturers. Burning sanitary products is difficult, requiring a decent fire, not just a cigarette lighter, and they don't compost well.

◆

*Jean Sinclair, 33, nurse and biologist, Cambridge, UK*

(*Schistosoma haematobium* and *S. mansoni*) and America (*Schistosoma mansoni*) are slow penetrators. Since it takes at least ten minutes to get through the skin, a quick splash across a suspect stream should do you no harm; vigorous towelling dry after bathing also kills any parasites caught in the act of skin penetration. Unfortunately Oriental schistosomiasis, *Schistosoma japonicum*, which occurs in parts of China, Taiwan, Vietnam, the Philippines, and two remote valleys in central Sulawesi, penetrates within a few minutes and is altogether a much nastier parasite.

- When in bilharzia country, and you are bathing, swimming, paddling, or wading in freshwater that you think may be risky, try to get out of the water within ten minutes. Then dry off thoroughly and vigorously with a towel; this will kill any parasites on their way in through your skin.

- Avoid bathing or paddling on shores within 200 meters of African villages or places where people use the water a great deal, especially reedy shores or where there is a lot of waterweed.

- If your bathing water comes from a source that may be contaminated with bilharzia, try to ensure that the water is taken from the lake in the early morning and stored snail-free, otherwise it should be filtered or have Dettol or Cresol added.

- Bathing early in the morning carries a lesser risk for bilharzia than bathing in the last half of the day.

- If you have been exposed to bilharzia parasites, arrange a screening blood test *more* than six weeks but ideally within twelve weeks of your last contact with suspect water.

- Bilharzia is never acquired from sea bathing.

There is another hazard of tropical rivers and bathing in them; this is onchocerciasis or river blindness. This is a problem in much of tropical sub-Saharan Africa between 19°N and 17°S, and it also occurs in parts of Central and tropical South America. This unpleasant worm is transmitted near to fast-flowing rivers through the bites of small biting blackflies, *Simulium damnosum*. These pestilential flies are a nuisance even in regions (like Asia) where river blindness is absent. Sand-fly bites cause big, very itchy lumps in the skin, often with a bloody speck at the center. River blindness has a variety of manifestations, since it invades many parts of the body, but in travelers and expatriates the worms most commonly make the skin incredibly itchy, and the itching is usually confined to a single limb or only the arms or legs. People need to have had extremely heavy infestations for many years before the eyes are threatened. Keep these daytime biters off with long loose clothes and a DEET-based insect repellent applied to any exposed skin.

To avoid flooding a Vietnamese bathroom, check the wash basin. In the absence of a waste pipe, take the bucket from beside the loo, and place it under the basin before washing. You will need the contents for flushing the loo—but remember to reposition the bucket beneath the basin before washing again; it's easy to forget.

♦

*Angela Rowe, 49, musician/IT worker, Swansea Valley, Wales*

If you want to bathe outdoors and there are lots of people about, it is possible to bathe modestly by putting on a sarong or *lungi*. This is a tube of cotton cloth that is wide enough to cover all essentials so that you can bathe comprehensively but modestly under a village water-spout in full view. For women, a long wraparound skirt can be used in the same way. Such garments will dry quickly in the midday sun along with your freshly washed underwear.

Bathing indoors has some advantages. In Indonesia each bathroom has a *bak mandi*, a water tank used to wash the bottom after using the toilet, flush the toilet, and also for bathing. The all-purpose technique is to scoop from the *bak mandi*. It is not a bath to climb into. Travelers often upset their Indonesian hosts by washing in the *bak mandi*, thereby polluting it and making it necessary to empty and clean the whole thing. In much of Southeast Asia there are similar cool water tanks. Water taken straight from a sun-baked tank on the roof would scald the bather, so often it is stored in huge terra-cotta pots inside the bathroom.

———— ✦ ✦ ————

Having a good wash can demand some subtlety, but cleaning wonders can be achieved, in the privacy of a very small tent, by squatting over a small dish of water and using a disposable cloth, soap, and preferably a close friend to scour your back. Start before sunset (with its attendant frost or mosquitoes) and begin at the savory end of your person, the lips. Then systematically work your way down. If you wish to use the cloth ever again, keep green ones for the upper part of your lovely body, and blue for bottoms. Finally hang the cloths out to dry, which they do even in a heavy frost at night, and once dry (usually about an hour after dawn), you can pack them into separate polyethylene bags. When they begin to get a bit fruity, just burn them and use new ones.

◆

*Dr. Jim Waddell, 66, retired consultant internal physician, Cirencester, UK*

When I was about fourteen years old, I went to Paris on a school trip. We stayed in a cheap hotel, and the double room that Anne and I shared contained two beds and—behind a skimpy curtain—a toilet, wash basin, and a useful little footbath. We thought this was marvelously civilized; we'd spend our summer days tramping around the hot city and come back grubby and footsore, when there was usually a queue for the shower. Our teacher laughed when he heard us enthuse about the footbath. "It's a *bidet* not a footbath! It's for washing your bottom after you've used the lavatory…"

At high altitude, daytime sunshine can be warming but temperatures plummet after dark in the mountains. During the misguided invasion of Tibet led by Younghusband in 1903, a British "officer so forgot himself as he bedded down for his first night in Tibet that he put his teeth into a tumbler of water. In the morning he reached for the tumbler and found it frozen solid, his dentures in the midst like a quail in aspic." This could happen to your toothbrush, too, if you leave it soaking in water

---

★ ★ ★

Dark cloth dries quicker in the sun than a light-colored one; a green towel is a good travel item.

♦

*John Hatt, 51, traveler and publisher, London, UK*

---

overnight in the high Andes or Himalayas. In these kinds of climates you may not want to do much washing at all, and there is some sense in developing a technique for minimal hygiene.

## *Tips*

➢ Make sure you wash your hands with soap and water after visiting any public toilet and before eating: your microbes won't harm you but other peoples' will. Attention to personal hygiene is more important when traveling than it is at home.

➤ Keeping your fingernails cut short will make them easier to keep clean. The speed that fingernails (and hair) grow depends upon environmental temperatures. Adventurers in the Arctic and Antarctic may not need to cut their nails for many months, while in the tropics they seem to need cutting every few days. Pack some nail clippers if traveling to warm climates.

➤ Malaria mosquitoes love sweaty feet, so a shower before dusk will reduce the bite rate.

➤ Take local advice before bathing outdoors.

➤ In tropical Africa, one of the most dangerous animals is the hippopotamus. They come out of the rivers to graze at dusk and during overcast days, so beware if you are bathing in the river or strolling along the riverbank. If you disturb them and are between them and the river—their refuge—they may flatten you in their panic to get back into the water.

➤ In sub-Saharan Africa if you are on the riverbank you may be on the menu. Watch out for Nile crocodiles. They eat about 1,000 Africans a year.

➤ Glance around before entering outside shower cubicles; they may be already occupied.

➤ Avoid stepping on stingrays, when bathing in South

> ———— ★ ★ ————
>
> I went to shower in the makeshift cubicle under a tree, in the remote Luangwa Valley, Zambia. There was a snake curled up inside: thick, grayish, about a yard long. It left through the reed wall as swiftly as I left through the space that acted as the door.
>
> ◆
>
> *Chris McIntyre, 33, guidebook author, tour operator, and safari addict, London, UK*

American rivers, by shuffling along in the water; this disturbs these fish, and they will swim away before you inadvertently step on them.

➤ Never dive headfirst into unknown turbid waters. It is always safer to jump.

➤ Plan where you will put the soap when bathing in rivers, otherwise it is likely to float off downstream and away out of reach.

➤ In Southeast Asia, scoop bathing water onto you from the water tank; don't climb into it or rinse your feet in it.

➤ If using an outside bathroom in the tropics, you may wish to avoid bathing around 6 P.M. when mosquitoes are at their hungriest; showering just before they gather at dusk is the best time.

➤ If you are renting a cheap hotel room that boasts en suite facilities, step into the bathroom—before the room boy leaves—to check for smells and listen awhile for drips. Water music from leaking plumbing can cause insomnia, and the smells from some facilities can be so overpowering as to make you wish they weren't en suite.

---

—— ★ ★ ——

I asked, in Calcutta, for the bathroom and was ushered into a room that was absolutely bare, apart from the concrete floor and a bucket of water. "But I wanted the loo, not a bath." I said. My hostess took me back into the room and pointed to a small hole in the wall and a long straw brush. Yes, one crapped on the floor and then had to brush the turds out into the hole with the brush, using the bucket of water to lubricate the process as well as wash the hands (and the bottom of course), or even take a shower.

◆

*Alan Smith, Australian development worker, Myanmar*

➢ Wash basins in cheap hotels often lack a plug. Universal sink plugs are available, otherwise half a squash ball works well. As a last resort, a scrumpled bit of plastic shopping bag will suffice.

The guest house in Darjeeling had no hot water, and the autumn chill that hung over the Himalayan foothills discouraged anything more than a washcloth bath, but for some reason just shy of masochism I decided to take a "shower" the way the locals did, by dipping a bucket into a cistern and pouring water over my head. The first bucket was bone chilling, but after that shock I hardly felt the rest, and at the end of a good scrubbing every nerve ending danced. I was so invigorated the day took on a new crispness, and I repeated the ritual every day for a week. That first bucket never felt good, but after bathing I felt alive in ways no other kick-start could accomplish.

◆

*Larry Habegger, 47, writer and editor, San Francisco, California*

# Chapter 15

## CHILDREN
### KEEPING LITTLE ONES HEALTHY

"That's not a toilet! I'm not going to wee in there. Can't we live
in a house with a proper toilet—a proper sit-down toilet?"

*—Alexander Howarth, aged three, on arriving
in his new home in rural Nepal*

———

*C*hildren are adaptable animals but unfamiliar lavatories
can intimidate them: children's fertile imaginations can
make all manner of things lurk in the shadows within. A
good, powerful flashlight might persuade a reluctant child into
a dark toilet, but even so, once inside, many children will be
scared of falling into the hole of a squat toilet. When my oldest
son was three, we went to live in a village on an island in the
middle of Nepal's biggest river. He was intimidated by our outside squat toilet and coped by perfecting the technique of peeing into it from outside the door, or using a potty. When he
needed to open his bowels, he and I developed the technique
of squatting together. He'd squat over the hole with me behind
him for support. He still gave many a backward glance at the
intimidating chasm beneath his bum.

Even as children grow older and bolder, the squatty can just
be too large for a child to squat over; they need more help than
with a pedestal WC—and "training seats" are useless. A potty
thus might be handy even if, under normal circumstances, the
child has outgrown one; they are useful if the child can't manage to squat or if the toilet is a long, dark walk outside.

Disposable diapers are a tremendous boon to parents because they absorb so much more than terry-cloth diapers, but they can be very expensive if purchased in developing countries: they are usually at least twice the price they are at home. And disposal is a problem. I have tried burning them, pouring on kerosene and igniting them and even wondered whether the solution was to wrap them around some Semtex explosive—they are indestructible and the only sensitive thing to do with soiled disposable diapers is to bury them, deep. Putting them into the hotel garbage will often result in them being dumped somewhere where dogs will play with them, and they'll end up blowing around the streets. Consider using at least some cloth diapers; cleaning of the diaper is made easier and less unpleasant if disposable liners are used since these can be flushed away with the poop. Families who are staying in one place for a few days will be able to wash cloth diapers, and one way to detoxify a soiled diaper is to soak it in diluted liquid bleach before washing. Bleach is readily available in a surprising number of quite remote destinations, so it is not necessary to bring soaking solution from home. It is risky stuff to have in your luggage and it is heavy yet it will be inexpensive when bought abroad.

In much of Asia, toddlers don't use diapers, but run around bare-bottomed; when they do "perform" there is usually a dog around to lick the child clean. If there's no dog then there are other resources: I once saw an older brother wiping a younger's bottom with a rock.

♦

*Brian Peniston, 47, international conservation and development worker, Nepal*

The risk of intestinal problems is great in travelers, particularly in regions with fewer resources than at home. The risks to traveling children are even greater, since they love exploring unhygienic places and they also have less immunity than adults. Some cautious physicians would even suggest that children under three years of age should not travel to areas where filth-to-mouth disease is rife. The highest-risk regions are probably tropical Latin America and the Indian subcontinent, including Nepal, and here small children will have a greater than 50–50 chance of getting some fairly unpleasant form of diarrhea or dysentery, and they also risk other filth-to-mouth diseases including typhoid and hepatitis A.

Children need to be fully immunized before travel; immunization is actually more important in traveling families than those who stay at home. In countries (like the U.S.) where there is a successful immunization program, there is a low risk of contracting infectious disease, because there are few suscepti-

Was it supper the night before or the rocking motion of the narrow-gauge railcar? Our two children, aged one and three, started diarrhea as soon as we left Guayaquil. We ran out of diapers and toilet paper. Others were suffering too—from both ends. The train toilet soon became blocked, but Ecuadorians take such journeys in their stride. Toilet paper was handed round. Jokes flew as everyone shared their resources, and advice. Every time the train broke down, we all used the countryside; seventeen hours later, we chugged into Quito at midnight—parents exhausted but children miraculously recovered.

◆

*Jane Vincent-Havelka, over 60, writer/photographer and former traveling mother, London, Ontario, Canada*

ble people around to pass these infections on. In many developing countries immunization coverage may be only 20 to 50 percent and so the pool of possible infectors is great.

The younger a child is, the more they risk serious complications of infectious disease. Infants and toddlers get sicker faster than older children, and may become very unwell indeed if they contract bacilliary dysentery. It is also more difficult to identify the source of the problem. Is she unwell, bored, anxious? Parents of small children who travel to less-hygienic countries must read and prepare well before departure; in particular, they must know about oral rehydration therapy and about the diagnosis of dehydration.

Apart from avoiding travelers' diarrhea, the biggest challenge when traveling with children is entertaining them and keeping them happy. The most successful project for travelers of any age over about three is to write a "diary." Toward the end of the day, or when waiting around for a bus, get out an exercise book and colored pens and encourage each child to write or draw so that each day they put something on paper. Some will draw whatever they are obsessed with at the time (like castles, airplanes, or dinosaurs), some will draw what they can see, some will record a highlight of the day, like mum slipping in a puddle. Depending upon the age and motivation of the family, you can decorate this with pressed flowers or leaves, or later with photographs. Some parents get the child to dictate what is to be written in the diary while the parent acts as scribe. But the important thing is to get something that the child "owns" down on paper most days of the journey; even a dinosaur drawing will elicit fond memories, and later the child will feel proud of the "book" they have written.

## Tips

➤ Traveling children must be fully immunized since they are likely to come into contact with unimmunized people and thus their risk of infectious disease is higher.

➤ Small children can be scared by dark, unfamiliar toilets (many have no functioning light in less-developed countries), and parents need to go with them. Even during the day, carrying a flashlight will help illuminate the gloom of a basic toilet.

➤ Wise parents travel with toilet paper and also some Wet Wipes.

➤ Children often carry a favorite toy on their visit to the loo; beware that it doesn't fall into the *shaucht*.

➤ Families with toddlers who are going to live in the developing world should endeavor to find out what kinds of loos are likely to be available. We took a toilet training seat to Nepal only to discover it was useless on our outside squat toilet. Potties, on the other hand, can be useful for older children who wouldn't use them at home; they avoid the need to stroll out into the hazardous mosquito-ridden tropical night.

A four-year-old patient's definition of diarrhea: "My bottom has got a cold— it keeps sneezing!"

♦

JW-H

➤ When packing disposable diapers for your child, assume that she will get diarrhea and you will need more diapers than you'd use at home.

➤ Some greasy healing cream will soothe baby's bottom (and his parents') after diarrhea.

➤ Dispose of soiled diapers sensitively. Bury soiled disposable diapers if there is no alternative garbage disposal system.

➤ Keep a spare set of clothes in your day bag or flight carry-on bag, in case of unexpected emissions.

➤ Dark colored underwear is more travel-wise than white.

➤ It is worthwhile keeping a plastic bag in your pocket—traveling children puke a lot.

➤ Changing mats are useful for diaper changes and also—in a less clean or scratchy environment—to just put a baby down.

➤ Thermos flasks of boiling water have many uses for traveling families: making up formula milk or baby rice, scalding cups and plates, producing safe water, cleaning baby's bum, etc. Hot water is especially invaluable, if the child is at the stage of playfully tossing spoons or cups into the gutter.

In Nepal small children run around with nothing on below the waist. I was painting in a village and, as usual, people gathered around to watch the portrait unfold. Suddenly I felt warm rain falling on my leg: a little boy was peeing while he watched—all over me.

♦

*Jan Salter, 61,
British artist, Nepal*

➤ Baby pacifiers may be dangerous to small children traveling in unhygienic places. They often fall onto the floor and so become contaminated and then this filth is transferred into the baby's mouth. If the child uses a pacifier, secure it with tape to the child's clothing so that it cannot fall.

➤ True "mineral water" from a natural spring is too high in minerals for small babies to drink safely and should not be used for small infants except in the very short term where there is no alternative. Boiled tap water is safer.

➤ Peel it, boil it, cook it, or forget it, is the motto to remind you how to keep traveling children free from the squirts in high-risk regions.

➤ When traveling in the developing world with children, and even on an upmarket beach holiday, it is worth packing a couple of oral rehydration packets.

➤ Beware of buffet food— especially meat dishes— in even the plushest of international hotels.

➤ As with adults, rehydration is important therapy when diarrhea strikes. Any clear fluid will be healing, but mixtures of sugar and salt are absorbed best. If the child will not take ORS (see Chapter 6) then try adding a pinch of salt to a favorite sweet drink like cola.

> ———— ✦ ————

We were on holiday in Thailand, recuperating from a simpler life in Nepal. My two-year-old's eyes lit upon the rubbery chicken sausages on display on the breakfast buffet. He devoured eight with gusto. At about 2 A.M. he awoke with hallucinations of snakes in his bed. A high fever was the cause of the hallucinations, and bacilliary dysentery was the cause of the fever. I gave him lots to drink, some acetaminophen (to lower his high temperature,) and sponged him cool. He recovered over the next two days and soon wanted more of those hotel sausages.

◆

*JW-H*

➤ The first sign of early dehydration is a dry mouth and tongue.

➤ Seek medical help promptly if in doubt or if the child is becoming too drowsy to drink.

➤ The secret of happy family travels is to have some instant entertainments always on hand in case of delays or queues. I suggest one or two from the following list: small toys such as cars, little figures or plastic animals, balloons, pens and paper, playing cards, favorite storybooks, inflatable beach-ball, a Frisbee.

➤ It can be difficult to be sure whether a child is really ill or just a little tired or off-color; taking the child's temperature can often help sort this out, and wise parents will travel with a thermometer.

➤ When traveling with children under the age of about five years, it is handy to carry some Tylenol (acetaminophen) syrup or chewable tablets from home. Acetaminophen, which is called paracetamol in much of the rest of the world, is widely available but many child formulations are rather unpalatable.

➤ The English are pretty stuffy and unaccommodating of children. If you need to eat out in England, Italian restaurants (or establishments run by southern Europeans) are among the most child-friendly.

We'd planned an eight-day trek with three-month-old Harriet in the middle hills of Nepal, through moderate altitudes along a forested ridge that crossed a road halfway. The first night we reached the misty, damp campsite where it transpired that a (rare) rogue porter had run off with his load including all the disposable diapers. The thief must have been disappointed because our senior porter later found them down a ravine. We set out the next morning thinking nothing else could go wrong, but unseasonal and inauspicious rain clouds clung to our ridge; Harriet was dry under a poncho but she developed a cough. Halfway we decided to hitch back to Kathmandu where Harriet quickly recovered from mild bronchiolitis. Sometimes plans have to change when traveling with children; ensure there is a backup plan, and plenty of diapers.

◆

*Dr. Matthew Ellis, 41, pediatrician and co-author of*
Your Child's Health Abroad, *Bristol, UK*

## Chapter 16

# SENIOR TRAVELERS
## ASSESSING SPECIAL NEEDS

It is at times like these that you realise the blessings of a good thick
skirt. Had I paid heed to the advice of many people in England, who
ought to have known better, and did not do it themselves, and
adopted masculine garments, I should have been spiked to the bone,
and done for. Whereas, save for a good many bruises, here I was
with the fulness of my skirt tucked under me, sitting on nine
ebony spikes some twelve inches long, in comparative
comfort, howling lustily to be hauled out.

—*Mary Kingsley, at the bottom of an*
*African animal trap (1893)*

---

*T*raveling by rail from Cambridge to London, I fell into
conversation with the older gentleman sitting opposite
me. He was an architect who'd been involved in
designing British Rail facilities. He was disgruntled when he
returned from the high-tech loo. "I can't see so well without my
glasses, and I wasn't sure what button to press! The designer
ought to be shot!"

When I went to investigate I could sympathize. Here is
what you do on the new West Anglia Great Northern Railway
trains. Firstly find the button marked <>. It is outside at the
level of your belly button. Press to open the big curved door.
Then inside just left of the wash basin, find the button >< to
close; then press the flashing button with a key symbol on it to
lock the door. Then when your organs have been duly evacuated,
find the flush button, the water button, the hot air drying but-

ton, then the open door button marked <>. If you manage all this you'll be awarded an honorary Ph.D.

Operating the toilet door did seem so unnecessarily complex that I wondered what other challenges travel presents to older travelers or those who have even the mild handicap of less-than-good eyesight. With increasing years, it becomes increasingly necessary to prepare properly for any trip, especially if the trip is to be somewhat strenuous. Failing to do this before going trekking left me with knees so very stiff, swollen, and painful that I could not use a squat toilet for weeks, and that—in Nepal—was disastrous. Even peeing from on high in a squat toilet splatters everything and you need a below-waist shower after every visit.

Preparations need to include not only physical conditioning but careful packing too. Have you remembered the contact lens solution, the hormone replacements, and any other regular medicines that you take? A seventy-eight-year-old man consulted me recently. He was down from the north of England visiting relatives, and he'd forgotten to pack any of the seven different drugs he needed to take. Worse, he had absolutely no idea what the medicines were, or what they were for. Whatever your age, it is sensible to have a note of any regular medication and keep that note somewhere different from the drugs themselves in case your luggage is lost. When traveling abroad, ensure you know the generic name of your medication, since

> Before I go trekking, I do 100 step-ups on a dining chair; 50 leading with one leg and 50 leading with the other. I do this each day for several days before the trip. This strengthens my thigh muscles to make the first days of the trek less painful, and it also protects my knees from injury.
>
> ◆
>
> *Jan Salter, 61,*
> *British artist, Nepal*

trade names are not international and are rarely intelligible to doctors of other nations who may end up prescribing replacement medicines. By the time the seventy-eight-year-old came to see me his legs were grossly swollen and he was in heart failure, unnecessarily.

Before anyone travels it is important to assess the risks being taken by the particular person in the particular chosen destination. Someone who is taking medicines for heart disease may be more at risk, for example, from electrolyte disturbance in case of diarrhea. Diuretic medicines encourage fluid and electrolyte loss in a way not dissimilar from the fluid and electrolyte loss of diarrhea, and both mechanisms can leave the body depleted of potassium. Blood tests can confirm whether the electrolyte balance is all right, but it may be that you are in a region where reliable laboratory facilities do not exist. Traveling with oral rehydration packets is one obvious precaution, another is being extra cautious about avoiding filth-to-mouth diseases, and even considering whether a trip to a high-risk destination is right for you. If planning a trip to

Five of us celebrated our fiftieth birthdays by different strenuous treks in Nepal; we only discovered this when meeting later. Since then I've trekked in Africa, Irian Jaya, the Himalayas, and the Hindu Kush. A friend celebrated her sixtieth by climbing Kilimanjaro, and I by a month-long pilgrimage to Mt. Kailas, Tibet with a pass at 18,600 feet. I know quite a few over-sixties who have no intention of slowing down yet, but we work at our fitness, and make these challenges a priority in our lives. Mental preparation and stamina are as important as the physical. And we are lucky to have the basic good health which allows us to do this.

◆

*Jane Vincent-Havelka, over 60, writer/photographer, London, Ontario, Canada*

Europe, for example, it will be helpful to know that the risk of diarrheal disease is lower in winter than in summer, and that the risk of the squits striking in northern Europe is perhaps 8 percent (less than one in ten travelers will suffer in any one trip), whereas for southern Europe it is around 30 percent, one-third.

Some people have suffered from a blood clot (thrombosis) and have to take an anticoagulant such as warfarin for some months. Traveling far and to remote regions while taking anticoagulants may be ill-advised. Intramuscular travel immunizations are also not advised since this will lead to uncomfortable bleeding within the muscle. The regular blood tests will not necessarily be possible and in case of an accident, disastrous bleeding may be the result. Further, someone who has had a clot in the past, risks another whenever undertaking a journey that necessitates sitting for more than six hours. Consider the risks and realize that medical facilities are not uniform the world over, nor are the risks of travel to different destinations.

Traveling overnight in desert Rajasthan, we did eventually halt briefly in a main street. The public "toilet" consisted of the long wall to the left against which a line of male backs made satisfied Sch-sch-weppes noises, and for me—lone female—the wall to the right where I squatted midway between two streetlights and in imagined privacy relieved my bursting bladder.

◆

*Joan Gilchrist, 70, granny with incurable wanderlust, Birmingham, UK*

# Tips

➤ Anyone taking diuretic ("water") tablets who suffers a

significant attack of diarrhea should seek medical help promptly if they start to feel dizzy on rising out of a chair or from bed. This is a sign of dehydration (see Chapter 6) and probably also indicates the loss of essential electrolytes.

➤ All travelers should know about self-treatment of travelers' diarrhea with oral rehydration solution, and it makes sense to travel with some ORS packets (see page 40).

➤ Those who suffer from diabetes are also likely to become more unwell than nondiabetic travelers when they get diarrhea and should seek a medical consultation if they feel unwell. It is all right for diabetics to take ORS (despite the fact it contains glucose). Those whose diabetes is controlled with tablets may temporarily need insulin by injection or via an intravenous drip if the diarrhea is severe.

On returning from your holiday, friends invariably ask, "What were the bathrooms like?" There was one in Vietnam with taps to the bath on the opposite side of the bathroom. But the very best places have no bathrooms at all, not even a hole in the ground, until you dig it. Planning your first trip to a wilderness area, the very first thing you must do, especially if you are over fifty, is to take squatting lessons. These can be had at any gymnasium or yoga class. If you don't master prolonged squatting, think again about whether you should risk that trip.

◆

*Dr. Jim Waddell, 66, internal medicine physician, Cirencester, UK*

➤ Some ongoing medical conditions make long-haul trips or travel to very remote regions unwise. Ask your doctor what is sensible. Bad backs, for example, are made more painful by long car journeys and probably also by long jarring bus rides.

➢ Take plenty of any medicines that you need and preferably pack them in two different bags in case a suitcase gets lost or delayed. Also travel with a list of all medicines you take, their generic names, and the exact doses. Never assume that you will be able to replenish your tablets at your destination. Similarly, not every country can provide reliable medical laboratory services for routine blood tests, etc.

➢ When planning a long, intercontinental journey that you expect to be tiring or stressful, consider buying a business-class ticket. This costs more but provides a comfortable, uncrowded waiting area before boarding, and much more space and more attentive service in flight. You thus arrive fresher and are less likely to feel that you need to recover before starting to enjoy your travel experience.

➢ If business-class travel is not feasible, ensure—at least—that your flight times are convenient. Many cut-priced tickets have you flying on unpleasant, sleep-depriving schedules.

➢ Bring along an extra pair of eyeglasses or a copy of your eyeglass prescription; replacements bought in the developing world can be remarkably inexpensive.

➢ Those who have difficulty squatting should do some limbering up exercises before travel; ladies can invest in a packet of disposable Whizzys (see page 100).

➢ If some illness strikes just before your planned trip, give serious thought to whether it would be better to postpone the trip. It is no fun traveling ill, and doctors at your destination are likely to have very different, unfamiliar consultation styles, which may not be very reassuring.

➤ Try to make a hard, rational assessment of your capabilities before any trip and make sure you are up to it. Get fit for your trip because aging bodies need more training for unfamiliar activities. I have met many trekkers, more than twenty years my senior, yet managing the physical demands better than I, but it is clear that these travelers have invested a lot of time in keeping in condition.

➤ People over the age of seventy-five may find it difficult (or at least more expensive) to rent a car or arrange travel insurance. Allow plenty of time for such arrangements; plan well ahead.

---

A keen young British officer in France during World War II, jumped out on a sentry.

"What would you have done if I'd been a Jerry?"

"I've just done it, Sir."

◆

*Joseph Wilson, 79, veteran Irish Guardsman, Surrey, UK*

# Chapter 17

## HOMECOMING
### YOU'VE RETURNED,
### ARE YOU HEALTHY?

Simagaul arrived with his *charriot-aux-boeufs* for the last time. He
asked for a third course of antibiotics for VD, but I was unsure
whether he had actually got it again or only intended to…. We
loaded the cart with rucksacks and made our final walk through the
forest of the Canyon Grande. Armand guided us out across the
savannah to a junction of two dirt tracks, about eight miles from
camp, where a bush taxi passed at 11 A.M. each day. He picked some
custard apples and ate them with us before he departed. It had been
a good expedition. I sat in the shade, so sad to be leaving, but
musing greedily on the culinary delights awaiting us in Diégo-Suarez.
It would not take me long to replace the fifteen pounds of fat I had
lost during my two and a half months in Madagascar.

– *Jane Wilson*, Lemurs of the Lost World

———

The vast majority of travelers return from their exotic
adventures feeling very well, yet they often have concerns about tropical hitchhikers. Feeling well does not
necessarily dispel the thought that some weird infection might
be lurking within, soon to break out and overwhelm them. Is
this likely? The answer is "no." Fortunately, almost all tropical
diseases and infections will cause some kind of symptoms so
that you are alerted and can take yourself to the doctor for
treatment. And those that don't cause symptoms rarely need
treatment. There are, of course, a few exceptions and it is
worth mentioning those to be aware of.

Perhaps the most common health problem, especially after

returning from a long, perhaps life-changing trip, is connected with mood. It can be quite an anticlimax coming back, realizing that life has gone on perfectly well without you. You may need to find a job, somewhere to live; you may find it hard initially to find kindred spirits to talk to. Depression can creep up on you. Be aware that "post-trip blues" are common, and the best treatment is to link up with other returned travelers and talk about your feelings. And if your moods are unbearably low much of the time, you are not sleeping well, or you are tearful, seek medical help. Usually it is a passing phenomenon and you'll get back to normal, only richer for the experience.

Malaria can catch travelers unaware so that they become rapidly ill. Sub-Saharan Africa is a common place to contract malaria, whether or not you have taken precautions against the disease. Realize when and where you might contract malaria. Symptoms begin at least a week after the first bite and usually within three months of return, but possibly up to a year of leaving a malarious region. Seek medical help urgently if you become feverish with aches and pains, and you think you could have malaria.

Did you put yourself at risk of HIV on your travels? Symptoms are rare initially but a screening blood test will tell you whether you have become infected. And similarly bilharzia, the disease acquired from paddling or swimming in infected freshwater in Africa and parts of tropical South America (see pages 103–105), may cause no symptoms but a blood test done more than six weeks from your last possible exposure will tell you if you need treatment.

Apart from those exceptions, almost all other infections will cause telltale symptoms. Those who have been traveling independently in countries with poor sanitation often pick up a worm or two, but in small numbers they are most unlikely to harm you. Probably the first you will know of their presence is passing one once it comes to the end of its life (see Chapter 11). It doesn't matter whether you get these treated or not, but if you are squeamish about the possibility of carrying worms, organize a stool test.

# *Tips*

➤ Remember the risk of serious malaria and seek medical help urgently (within twenty-four hours) if you fall ill within three months of returning from the tropics—even if you have taken your antimalarial tablets.

➤ Antimalarial tablets should be continued for at least four weeks after returning from your travels; they are not an absolute guarantee that you will avoid malaria, but if you are unlucky enough to get it, you are less likely to die of it.

➤ Other diseases imported from the tropics are unlikely to be serious, but seek a medical opinion if you notice a rash, an ulcer that refuses to heal, new lumps or bumps, or are unwell. Remind your doctor that you have been abroad.

➤ If you are feeling down after your trip, find a kindred spirit to talk to.

➤ Do not worry about your health on your return; if you feel well, you almost certainly are well.

In Madras we made our way among groups of men repairing nets in the sand, watching our step to avoid the steaming piles of human excrement (the beach is "dirty," we'd been warned), exchanging smiles and conversation with fishermen. A man wiping his behind in the surf rolled his *lungi* back to his knees and leapt up as we passed, saying "How are you, what is your name?" Rather than shake his proffered hand we tented ours in the traditional Hindu greeting, said "*Namaste*" ("I bow to the divine in you"), and continued our stroll.

◆

—*James O'Reilly and Larry Habegger,* Travelers' Tales India

# Chapter 18

## PACKING LIST AND MINIMAL MEDICAL KIT

*M*y first big trip to the developing world was in 1976, and I went weighed down with a ridiculous quantity of medicaments, most of which I gave away. Now I am older and wiser and these days when I travel I take very little. My recommended absolute minimum first-aid kit is:

- A good drying antiseptic (e.g., iodine or potassium permanganate)—don't take antiseptic cream. Remember skin infections are common in the tropics

- A few small dressings (Band-Aids plus some larger nonstick dressings and micropore tape to stick them on with). Scrapes and grazes need covering against flies and other insects

- Steristrips—tape for pulling the edges of large wounds together

- Insect repellent; malaria tablets; impregnated mosquito net

- Condoms (they also can be useful emergency water carriers)

- Sunscreen with a protection factor (SPF) of 15 or more

- Acetaminophen (paracetamol) or aspirin-soluble forms are good for gargling with when you have a sore throat

- Antifungal cream (e.g., Daktarin or Canesten) for athlete's foot and groin itches

- Greasy soothing cream or hemorrhoid treatment for the overexerted anus

- Ciprofloxacin antibiotic 500 mg x 6 (or Norfloxacin or Nalidixic Acid) for severe diarrhea

- Another broad-spectrum antibiotic like amoxycillin (for chest, urine, skin infections, etc.)

- A pair of fine pointed tweezers for removing thorns, coral fragments, caterpillar hairs, etc.

- Nail clippers or scissors

Here are few more hygiene-related items that you might need when traveling in less-developed regions:

- Reliable flashlight (preferably a headlight)

- Toilet paper

- Wet wipes

- Disposable cleaning cloths or a washcloth

- Large dark-colored (green, navy) bath towel and maybe a sarong

- Resealable plastic bags or at least a few plastic shopping bags (for vomit or soiled clothes)

- One or two good quality one-liter water bottles

- Iodine to purify the water (and also useful when diluted as an antiseptic) and vitamin C to improve the taste, or a water purification device

- Vacuum flask

- Oral rehydration packets—check that the cup or bottle that you carry is the correct volume for making up ORS

- A few Oxo stock (boullion) cubes for making savory drinks during diarrhea

- An oral rehydration "recipe" (see page 41)

- Plastic containers to mix rehydration solutions and carry liquids

- A fine-toothed comb (for lice) especially if traveling with children

- Women's sanitary items sealed in good waterproof container or plastic bags

- A list of any medicines you take with a note of their generic names

- Spare eyeglasses or eyeglasses prescription

- Immunization certificates

- At least one good, long novel

# Chapter 19

# RESOURCES AND REFERENCES

———

# *Books for Further Reading*

Arscott, David. *Sussex Privies: A Nostalgic Trip Down the Garden Path.* Newbury Berkshire, UK: Countryside Books, 1998.

Belamy, David. *Poo You and the Potoroo's Loo.* London, UK: Portland Press, 1997. Neat children's book about environmental responsibilities.

Bezruchka, Stephen, M.D. *Altitude Illness, Prevention, and Treatment.* Seattle: The Mountaineers, 1994. A helpful, accessible guide; essential reading for trekkers.

Bezruchka, Stephen, M.D. *The Pocket Doctor: A Passport to Healthy Traveling (3rd ed.).* Seattle, Washington: The Mountaineers, 1999. Covers preparations, precautions, and care while abroad. A sensible, helpful guide in a conveniently small format.

Centers for Disease Control. *Health Information for International Travel.* Atlanta, Georgia: CDC, 2000. Best English-language publication for international disease risks information, though hardly an entertaining read. Annually updated. Single copies are available from CDC (Attention Health Information), Center for Prevention Services, Division of Quarantine, Atlanta, GA 30333, USA.

Lewin, R. A. *Merde: Excursions into Scientific, Cultural and Socio-Historical Coprology*. New York: Random House.

Meyer, Kathleen. *How to Shit in the Woods: An Environmentally Sound Approach to a Lost Art*. Berkeley, California: Ten Speed Press, 1994. Practical advice for backcountry travel as well as environmental methods for keeping wild places pristine, esthetically and bacterially.

Newman, Eva. *Going Abroad: The Bathroom Survival Guide*. St. Paul, Minnesota: Marlor Press, 1997. A guide to unfamiliar toilets.

Pollard, A.J., and D.R. Murdoch. *The High Altitude Medicine Handbook*. Oxford, UK: Radcliffe Medical Press, 1997. Authoritative book, although a bit technical in places, written by two physicians who are also mountaineers.

Reyburn, Wallace. *Flushed with Pride: The Story of Thomas Crapper*. London: Pavilion Books, 1989.

Sullivan, Donald. *A Senior's Guide to Health Travel*. Franklin Lakes, New Jersey: Career Press, 1994.

Turner, Jean. *East Anglian Privies: A Nostalgic Trip Down the Garden Path*. Newbury Berkshire, UK: Countryside Books, 1998.

Warrell, David, and Sarah Anderson (eds.). *Expedition Medicine*. London: Profile Books and the Royal Geographical Society,

1998. All you need to know about health and illness on expeditions including how to build a latrine. Written by two senior expedition physicians. Warrell is professor at the Oxford University Medical School and a world authority on venomous creatures.

*Where to GO in the Great Outdoors.* Mountaineering Council of Scotland. 4A St Catherine's Rd, Perth PH1 5SE (send SAE), Phone 01738-638229, fax 01738-442095. Useful pamphlet for walkers in Britain.

Wilkerson, J.A., (ed.). *Medicine for Mountaineering.* Seattle: The Mountaineers, 1985. Somewhat overtechnical in places, but otherwise an excellent book; covers low-altitude wilderness medicine as well.

Wilson-Howarth, Jane. *Bugs, Bites and Bowels: Travel Health.* London: Cadogan Guides; Old Saybrook, Connecticut: The Globe Pequot Press, 1999. Accessible health information packed into a slim format, written by a physician who has practiced in the developing world for a decade. Contains instructive case histories to learn from. Probably the most readable of the health guides.

Wilson-Howarth, Jane, and Matthew Ellis. *Your Child's Health Abroad: A Manual for Travelling Parents.* Chalfont St. Peter, UK: Bradt Publications; Old Saybrook, Connecticut: The Globe Pequot Press, 1998. Comprehensive. Written by two physicians who are also widely traveled parents.

World Health Organization. *International Travel and Health: Vaccination Requirements and Health Advice.* Geneva,

Switzerland: World Health Organization Publications, 2000. Costs SFR 15 or US$13.50. Annually updated booklet; dry reading.

# Newsletters and Journals

*Planet Talk.* Lonely Planet Publications. PO Box 617, Hawthorn, VIC 3122, Australia or go@lonelyplanet.co.uk. Free. Quarterly. Usually carries travel health items.

*RoughNews* is a free newsletter that now usually carries travel health information and updates. 375 Hudson Street, New York, NY 10014. Fax 212-414-3395 or www.roughguides.com/travel.

*Traveling Healthy: Health Advice for the Global Traveler.* P.O. Box 13795, Milwaukee, WI 53213-0795, USA. Bimonthly.

*Wanderlust* bimonthly magazine which carries a two-page article on some aspect of travel health in each bimonthly issue. P.O. Box 1832, Windsor, Berkshire SL4 6YP, UK. Fax 00-44-1753-620474.

# Services and Organizations

Centers for Disease Control (CDC)
Atlanta, GA 30333 USA
Phone 404-332 4559 or 888-232-3228
Web site: www.cdc.gov
The CDC is the central source of travel health information in North America, with a touch-tone phone line and fax service. They publish each summer the invaluable *Health Information for International Travel.*

Connaught Laboratories
P.O. Box 187
Swiftwater, PA 18370 USA
Phone 800-822-2463
Connaught Laboratories will send a free list of specialist
tropical physicians in your state.

International Association for Medical Assistance to Travellers
(IAMAT)
736 Center Street
Lewiston NY 14092 USA
716-754-4883
A nonprofit foundation that provides lists of English-speaking
doctors abroad as well as foreign health information.

Canadian Department of Trade and Foreign Affairs
Phone 613-944-6788 or – 800-267-6788
Faxcall system 1-800-575-2500
Web site: http://www.dfait-maeci.gc.ca
Travel reports available via phone, fax and website..

# World Wide Web

Centers for Disease Control and Prevention
www.cdc.gov/travel
Includes a country by country list of immunizations and advice
on malaria risk.

Global Programme for Vaccines and Immunizations (GPV)
www.who.int/gpv-dvacc/travel.htm
Part of the World Health Organization, this web site provides

information on vaccination requirements and health advice for international travelers.

HealthLink
http://healthlink.mcw.edu/travel-medicine/
A travel medicine web site run by the medical College of Wisconsin. Free health newsletter. Details of major infectious diseases and information on where they are found, plus recommended vaccines and precautionary advice.

The Healthy Traveler
www.healthytraveler.com
On-line travel store, resources, and information for travelers, including safety and security, weather, medical organizations, etc. Available in English, Spanish, French, and German.

International Association for Medical Assistance to Travelers (IAMAT)
www.sentex.net/ iamat/
Advises travelers of health risks, geographical distribution of diseases, immunization requirements, as well as providing lists of English-speaking doctors throughout the world.

International Society of Travel Medicine
www.istm.org
The big organization for health professionals; not for the faint-hearted.

Lonely Planet Health Check
www.lonelyplanet.com/health/
Includes information on predeparture planning, keeping healthy on the road, diseases and ailments, and health links.

ProMED
www.promedmail.org:8080/promed/promed.folder.home
A global electronic reporting system for outbreaks of emerging infectious diseases. Contains current alerts, outbreak maps, and articles on travel health. Available in English, Portuguese, Spanish, Chinese, and Japanese.

Travel Health Information Service
http://travelhealth.com
Everything you need to travel—except the shots. Provides general prevention guidelines, breaking news, risk assessment by destination, as well as links to organizations, government sites, etc.

Travel Health
www.travelhealth.com
Offers extensive reports on health risks of any trip for a fee of $24.95.

Travel Health Online
www.tripprep.com/index.html
This web site provides health and safety information on more than 220 countries, including immunization recommendations, preventions, warnings, travel medical providers, and health concerns.

World Health Organization
www.who.int/ith/english/welcome.html

# Index

# INDEX OF CONTRIBUTORS

# ACKNOWLEDGMENTS

———

This little book started with a germ of an idea of Sean O'Reilly's, and he called me in Kathmandu to ask me to write about shitting abroad. That's not the kind of request I often receive, but that was the start of an enjoyable e-mail relationship with the editors and staff of Travelers' Tales. Larry Habegger and Susan Brady have been patient in fielding my innumerable queries, and James O'Reilly has come up with some excellent suggestions. It will be clear, though, that this work would have been impossible without the contributions from those who sent me their voices of experience. The vast majority came in response to a plea in *Wanderlust*, the British travel magazine for whom I write regularly, but I also received contributions from members of the Scientific Exploration Society of Great Britain, and from assorted friends and relations. I am indebted to Lyn Hughes, editor of *Wanderlust,* and Wendy Bentall, editor of *Sesame,* the SES newsletter. Thanks also to Rachel Galloway for help with communications.

I am also enormously grateful to my outlaw sister, Jill Sutcliffe, for thinking of the title of the book, and to my husband Simon Howarth, for proofreading and being his usual quiet, supportive self. Many of the tales within these pages were collected whilst we've traveled together over the past years. I also appreciate my parents' liberal views in tolerating a daughter who talks crap and writes filth.

# About the Author

Dr. Jane Wilson-Howarth graduated first in ecology and then organized a six-month-long expedition to the Himalayas to study lesser wildlife there. Interested in cave life, she soon discovered that a lot could be learned from the brown deposits animals leave behind, as well as from watching creatures themselves. She spent a couple of years at Oxford University studying rabbit parasites, then entered medical school where her friends called her the Shit Doctor because of a continuing interest in parasites and poo. On completion of her studies, she was awarded a B.M.—a bachelor of medicine degree; this is equivalent to the American M.D. qualification.

She organized two research trips to Madagascar where dunes of bat guano hid rare species of invertebrates unknown to science. She also watched and photographed attractive creatures, completing the first-ever study of the endangered crowned lemur in the wild; this involved meticulous observations, and—of course—examinations of their emanations. Her first book, *Lemurs of the Lost World*, describes the Madagascar expeditions. Field studies in Peru continued on the ecology of excreta, and she worked where mounds of subterranean guano seethed with fascinating crawlies, and where spelunkers risked catching histoplasmosis and rabies.

She has lived in Asia for most of the last eleven years, working on various community health projects in Sri Lanka, Indonesia, Pakistan, India, Bangladesh, and Nepal; some of this work involved screening people for worms and also encouraging villagers to build and use latrines. She now lives with her husband and two sons in England where she teaches and lectures on travel medicine, works as a general practitioner, and enjoys the luxury of a home with two flush loos. Her two travel health guides, *Bugs Bites & Bowels* (Cadogan Guides) and *Your Child's Health Abroad* (Bradt Publications), are published in the U.S. by Globe Pequot.

# TRAVELERS' TALES GUIDES

## LOOK FOR THESE TITLES IN THE SERIES

### FOOTSTEPS: THE SOUL OF TRAVEL

**A NEW IMPRINT FROM TRAVELERS' TALES GUIDES**

An imprint of Travelers' Tales Guides, the Footsteps series unveils new works by first-time authors, established writers, and reprints of works whose time has come…again. Each book will fire your imagination, disturb your sleep, and feed your soul.

### KITE STRINGS OF THE SOUTHERN CROSS
**A Woman's Travel Odyssey**
*By Laurie Gough*
*ISBN 1-885211-30-9*
*400 pages, $24.00, Hardcover*

### THE SWORD OF HEAVEN
**A Five Continent Odyssey to Save the World**
*By Mikkel Aaland*
*ISBN 1-885211-44-9*
*350 pages, $24.00, Hardcover*

### STORM
**A Motorcycle Journey of Love, Endurance, and Transformation**
*By Allen Noren*
*ISBN 1-885211-45-7*
*360 pages, $24.00, Hardcover*

## ℘PECIAL INTEREST

### THE FEARLESS SHOPPER:
**How to Get the Best Deals on the Planet**
*By Kathy Borrus*
*ISBN 1-885211-39-2, 200 pages, $12.95*

## THE GIFT OF RIVERS:
### True Stories of Life on the Water
*Edited by Pamela Michael*
*Introduction by Robert Hass*
*ISBN 1-885211-42-2, 256 pages, $14.95*

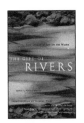

## SHITTING PRETTY:
### How to Stay Clean and Healthy While Traveling
*By Dr. Jane Wilson-Howarth*
*ISBN 1-885211-47-3, 200 pages, $12.95*

## THE GIFT OF BIRDS:
### True Encounters with Avian Spirits
*Edited by Larry Habegger & Amy G. Carlson*
*ISBN 1-885211-41-4, 352 pages, $17.95*

## TESTOSTERONE PLANET:
### True Stories from a Man's World
*Edited by Sean O'Reilly, Larry Habegger & James O'Reilly*
*ISBN 1-885211-43-0, 300 pages, $17.95*

## THE PENNY PINCHER'S PASSPORT
## TO LUXURY TRAVEL:
### The Art of Cultivating Preferred Customer Status
*By Joel L. Widzer*
*ISBN 1-885211-31-7, 253 pages, $12.95*

## DANGER!
**True Stories of Trouble and Survival**
*Edited by James O'Reilly, Larry Habegger & Sean O'Reilly*
*ISBN 1-885211-32-5, 336 pages, $17.95*

## FAMILY TRAVEL:
**The Farther You Go, the Closer You Get**
*Edited by Laura Manske*
*ISBN 1-885211-33-3, 368 pages, $17.95*

## THE GIFT OF TRAVEL:
**The Best of Travelers' Tales**
*Edited by Larry Habegger, James O'Reilly & Sean O'Reilly*
*ISBN 1-885211-25-2, 240 pages, $14.95*

## THERE'S NO TOILET PAPER...ON THE ROAD LESS TRAVELED:
**The Best of Travel Humor and Misadventure**
*Edited by Doug Lansky*
*ISBN 1-885211-27-9, 207 pages, $12.95*

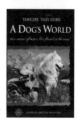

## A DOG'S WORLD:
**True Stories of Man's Best Friend on the Road**
*Edited by Christine Hunsicker*
*ISBN 1-885211-23-6, 257 pages, $12.95*

# ᗯOMEN'S TRAVEL

## A WOMAN'S PATH:
**Women's Best Spiritual Travel Writing**
*Edited by Lucy McCauley, Amy G. Carlson, and Jennifer Leo*
*ISBN 1-885211-48-1, 320 pages, $16.95*

## A WOMAN'S PASSION FOR TRAVEL:
**More True Stories from A Woman's World**
*Edited by Marybeth Bond & Pamela Michael*
*ISBN 1-885211-36-8, 375 pages, $17.95*

## SAFETY AND SECURITY FOR WOMEN WHO TRAVEL
*By Sheila Swan & Peter Laufer*
*ISBN 1-885211-29-5, 159 pages, $12.95*

## WOMEN IN THE WILD:
**True Stories of Adventure and Connection**
*Edited by Lucy McCauley*
*ISBN 1-885211-21-X, 307 pages, $17.95*

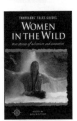

## A MOTHER'S WORLD:
**Journeys of the Heart**
*Edited by Marybeth Bond & Pamela Michael*
*ISBN 1-885211-26-0, 233 pages, $14.95*

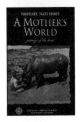

# $\mathcal{W}$OMEN'S TRAVEL

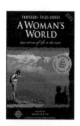

## A WOMAN'S WORLD:
**True Stories of Life on the Road**
*Edited by Marybeth Bond*
*Introduction by Dervla Murphy*
ISBN 1-885211-06-6
*475 pages, $17.95*

——— ★ ★ ★ ———
*Winner of the Lowell
Thomas Award for Best
Travel Book – Society of
American Travel Writers*

## GUTSY WOMEN:
**Travel Tips and Wisdom for the Road**
*By Marybeth Bond*
ISBN 1-885211-15-5, *123 pages, $7.95*

## GUTSY MAMAS:
**Travel Tips and Wisdom
for Mothers on the Road**
*By Marybeth Bond*
ISBN 1-885211-20-1, *139 pages, $7.95*

# $\mathcal{B}$ODY & SOUL

## THE ULTIMATE JOURNEY:
**Inspiring Stories of Living and Dying**
*James O'Reilly, Larry Habegger & Richard Sterling*
ISBN 1-885211-38-4
*336 pages, $17.95*

## ADVENTURE OF FOOD:
**True Stories of Eating Everything**
*Edited by Richard Sterling*
ISBN 1-885211-37-6
*336 pages, $17.95*

# ℬODY & SOUL

*Small Press Book
Award Winner and
Benjamin Franklin
Award Finalist*

## THE ROAD WITHIN:
### True Stories of Transformation
### and the Soul
*Edited by Sean O'Reilly, James O'Reilly
& Tim O'Reilly*
ISBN 1-885211-19-8, 459 pages, $17.95

## LOVE & ROMANCE:
### True Stories of Passion on the Road
*Edited by Judith Babcock Wylie*
ISBN 1-885211-18-X, 319 pages, $17.95

*Silver Medal Winner of the
Lowell Thomas Award for
Best Travel Book – Society of
American Travel Writers*

## FOOD:
### A Taste of the Road
*Edited by Richard Sterling
Introduction by Margo True*
ISBN 1-885211-09-0
467 pages, $17.95

## THE FEARLESS DINER:
### Travel Tips and Wisdom for Eating
### around the World
*By Richard Sterling*
ISBN 1-885211-22-8, 139 pages, $7.95

# ℭOUNTRY GUIDES

## IRELAND
### True Stories of Life on the Emerald Isle
*Edited by James O'Reilly, Larry Habegger, and Sean O'Reilly*
ISBN 1-885211-46-5, 368 pages, $17.95

# $\mathscr{C}$OUNTRY GUIDES

## AUSTRALIA
**True Stories of Life Down Under**
*Edited by Larry Habegger*
*ISBN 1-885211-40-6, 375 pages, $17.95*

## AMERICA
*Edited by Fred Setterberg*
*ISBN 1-885211-28-7, 550 pages, $19.95*

## JAPAN
*Edited by Donald W. George*
*& Amy Greimann Carlson*
*ISBN 1-885211-04-X, 437 pages, $17.95*

## ITALY
*Edited by Anne Calcagno*
*Introduction by Jan Morris*
*ISBN 1-885211-16-3, 463 pages, $17.95*

## INDIA
*Edited by James O'Reilly & Larry Habegger*
*ISBN 1-885211-01-5, 538 pages, $17.95*

# $\mathcal{C}$OUNTRY GUIDES

## FRANCE

*Edited by James O'Reilly, Larry Habegger*
*& Sean O'Reilly*
*ISBN 1-885211-02-3, 517 pages, $17.95*

## MEXICO

*Edited by James O'Reilly & Larry Habegger*
*ISBN 1-885211-00-7, 463 pages, $17.95*

—————★ ★ ★—————

***Winner of the Lowell***
***Thomas Award for Best***
***Travel Book – Society of***
***American Travel Writers***

## THAILAND

*Edited by James O'Reilly*
*& Larry Habegger*
*ISBN 1-885211-05-8*
*483 pages, $17.95*

## SPAIN

*Edited by Lucy McCauley*
*ISBN 1-885211-07-4, 495 pages, $17.95*

## NEPAL

*Edited by Rajendra S. Khadka*
*ISBN 1-885211-14-7, 423 pages, $17.95*

# COUNTRY GUIDES

## BRAZIL
*Edited by Annette Haddad & Scott Doggett*
*Introduction by Alex Shoumatoff*
*ISBN 1-885211-11-2*
*452 pages, $17.95*

— ★ ★ ★ —
**Benjamin Franklin**
**Award Winner**

# CITY GUIDES

## HONG KONG
*Edited by James O'Reilly, Larry Habegger & Sean O'Reilly*
*ISBN 1-885211-03-1, 439 pages, $17.95*

## PARIS
*Edited by James O'Reilly, Larry Habegger & Sean O'Reilly*
*ISBN 1-885211-10-4, 417 pages, $17.95*

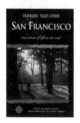

## SAN FRANCISCO
*Edited by James O'Reilly, Larry Habegger & Sean O'Reilly*
*ISBN 1-885211-08-2, 491 pages, $17.95*

# ᴄREGIONAL GUIDES

## HAWAI'I
### True Stories of the Island Spirit
*Edited by Rick & Marcie Carroll*
*ISBN 1-885211-35-X, 416 pages, $17.95*

## GRAND CANYON
### True Stories of Life Below the Rim
*Edited by Sean O'Reilly,*
*James O'Reilly & Larry Habegger*
*ISBN 1-885211-34-1, 296 pages, $17.95*

## SUBMIT YOUR OWN TRAVEL TALE

Do you have a tale of your own that you would like to submit to Travelers' Tales? We highly recommend that you first read one or more of our books to get a feel for the kind of story we're looking for. For submission guidelines and a list of titles in the works, send a SASE to:

### Travelers' Tales Submission Guidelines
330 Townsend Street, Suite 208, San Francisco, CA 94107

or send email to *guidelines@travelerstales.com*
or visit our Web site at **www.travelerstales.com**

You can send your story to the address above or via email to *submit@travelerstales.com*. On the outside of the envelope, ***please indicate what country/topic your story is about***. If your story is selected for one of our titles, we will contact you about rights and payment.

We hope to hear from you. In the meantime, enjoy the stories!